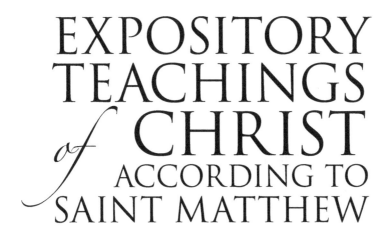

EXPOSITORY TEACHINGS *of* CHRIST ACCORDING TO SAINT MATTHEW

RAPHAEL ALADE ADENIYI

WESTBOW
PRESS®
A DIVISION OF THOMAS NELSON
& ZONDERVAN

WestBow Press books may be ordered through booksellers or by contacting:

WestBow Press
A Division of Thomas Nelson & Zondervan
1663 Liberty Drive
Bloomington, IN 47403
www.westbowpress.com
844-714-3454

Scripture quotations are from the King James Version of the Bible.

ISBN: 978-1-6642-1490-3 (sc)
ISBN: 978-1-6642-1492-7 (hc)
ISBN: 978-1-6642-1491-0 (e)

Library of Congress Control Number: 2020923903

Print information available on the last page.

WestBow Press rev. date: 12/04/2020

Foreword

Who would travel one-third of the way around the world only to live in a jam-packed furnished one-room apartment for several years to reach his vocational goal of being an educator and his spiritual goal of leading others to Christ? Only a man of God on a journey of faith.

Raphael Adeniyi made that journey from Ilé-Ifẹ̀, Nigeria, via Indianapolis, Indiana, to Calgary, Canada. It was during his six-year stay in Indianapolis that I first met Mr. Adeniyi in 2002. While in Indianapolis, Mr. Adeniyi earned his bachelor's degree in accounting from Martin University and was working on his master's degree in education at my alma mater, the University of Indianapolis. To qualify for a teaching credential in the state of Indiana, aspiring teachers must complete a supervised teaching experience in addition to the academic requirements. I served as Mr. Adeniyi's supervising teacher for his student teaching experience.

Even as he worked hard to overcome cultural challenges to become a teacher, Mr. Adeniyi was also serving as a pastor of Deeper Life Bible Church. Completing the requirements for his teaching credential was Raphael's vocational goal; however, his spiritual goal was to establish Deeper Life Bible Churches in all the major cities in Indiana, where he could bring the Good News of the gospel to others.

As Pastor Adeniyi worked to develop the lessons he would present to his congregation, he asked me to review his work for proofreading and spelling. To date, Raphael has written 265 lessons.

Pastor Adeniyi has gained thoughtful insights from his in-depth study of the Gospel of Saint Matthew. Even as a Roman Catholic, I have learned a great deal about the richness of Saint Matthew's writings from working on these lessons. I believe that ministers who are looking for aids in preparing their services, as well as any truth-seeking Christian, will benefit from the availability of these Bible study materials.

—Michael R. Cecil

Acknowledgments

This journey would not have been possible without the support of my family. My wife encouraged me to publish all of the Bible lessons I have written. She believes the lessons are very rich and will lead to the saving of souls. When I was a little bit discouraged about finding a publisher for the work, she spoke kind words that lifted my spirits and renewed my commitment to find the right publisher. I thank God that I listened to my wife and finally found WestBow Press to publish the book.

I also want to recognize the gifts of God in my family. God has blessed our family with three wonderful and unique sons. All the boys are great and easygoing individuals whom we have been able to parent with limited discipline. They are a pleasure to have around the house, as they never bother anyone. They are obedient sons, and I am grateful to God for these special sons.

I want to thank my parents, who brought me into this life. They were very good to me when I was growing up, and I had everything I wanted. My parents were Muslims, and their son being a Christian was not a problem for them. When I was under their care as a child, they allowed me to serve my God and never posed any threat to my faith. They financed my traveling to America for a better life; and, I cannot thank them enough for what they have done for me.

I am very grateful to my uncle, Pastor Emmanuel Oluyomi Atinaro (deceased), and my aunty, Elizabeth Omolara Atinaro. They were a godly couple, and both taught me practical Christianity when I lived with them while I attended the Polytechnics of Ibadan (Nigeria). Their genuine love of God strengthened me to take Christianity seriously. I was born again in their home in 1990. The experience of my salvation while in their home is still very vivid. I remember kneeling down beside my bed and asking the Lord to come into my heart and forgive me of all my sins. God bless the Atinaros for demonstrating practical Christianity to me within their family. I have followed the Christian family model I learned from your family in my own family.

Thanks to Deeper Life Bible Church! The church provided spiritual training for me at the very beginning of my coming to know the Lord as Savior. I received spiritual instruction that helped me mature as a believer and become an independent and true follower of the Lord, Jesus Christ. God has blessed Deeper Life Bible Church with faithful and committed leaders who are very effective in counseling converts who are coming to faith in Christ.

I was privileged, as a young Christian growing up, to have serious and dynamic spiritual mentors around me. Those leaders became role models for me in their lifestyles, in their methods of delivering Christian messages, and in their comportment. These men of God, whom I looked up to in the faith, challenged me to follow Christ, as I strove to be a faithful and serious servant of God. Some of my mentors are Pastor William Folorunsho Kumuyi (general superintendent of Deeper Life Bible Church), Pastor Seyi Olofintuyi, Pastor Gabriel Omobolanle Alabi, Sister Dorcas Alabi, Pastor Israel Omotade, and Pastor Emmanuel Ijaodola, among other great people of God.

I want to thank God for a man He brought into my life. God allowed me to have Mr. Michael Cecil as a field supervisor during my student teaching at Arsenal Technical High School in Indianapolis. Mr. Cecil is a detailed individual and a perfectionist. I am glad God sent this man my way, because he has taught me a lot, and I aspire to be like him in my writings. Mr. Cecil and I have had an unbroken relationship since my student teaching experience in 2002. I have always relied on him to check my Bible lessons for me, because I know he pays close attention to detail and simply wants the best for me. My prayer is that the Lord will sustain my relationship with Mr. Cecil and give him a long life.

Finally, I am grateful to God for allowing me to write Bible lessons on the Gospel according to Saint Matthew. The lessons were written under the inspiration of the Holy Spirit. I have never forced any lessons to be written on my own. When I am inspired, God sheds light on what He wants me to write, and the lesson becomes very easy, because the whole picture of what to write is already in my mind. The entire lesson just comes together, and all the parts connect. For God to use me to do this kind of work is truly a mind-boggling and humbling experience for me, because I am the least person who should be privileged to do this kind of assignment.

REACHING THE SPIRITUAL PLATFORM THAT WILL SAVE YOUR MARRIAGE FROM DIVORCE

Text: Matthew 1:19–20

Lesson Introduction: The attitudes and dispositions that believers have toward marriage and family are remarkably different than those of nonbelievers. Genuine salvation in Christ allows believers in Christ to demonstrate those virtues exhibited by Christ when He was in the world. In Malachi 2:16, the prophet tells us that the Almighty God hates putting away. In other words, God hates divorce. He wants spouses to reach the spiritual platform where they know how to forgive and forget. He wants each spouse to cover the nakedness of their partner in order not to subject the partner involved to the shame or ridicule of society. The truth of the matter is that we cannot boldly declare that we know Christ if our marriage is in shambles or we have divorced because of what we consider to be irreconcilable differences.

BREAKDOWN OF THE STUDY

1. Reaching the peak of perfection
2. Rising above public perspectives or positions to issues
3. Relying on positions that protect your partner

REACHING THE PEAK OF PERFECTION

Matthew 1:19; 5:48; Luke 1:5–6; 2:25; 1 Peter 3:16; 2:9;
Job 1:1; Acts 10:2; Mark 6:20; Genesis 6:9

Joseph was a believer in God and was referred to as a just man (Matthew 1:19). Being a just man means he was not a baby believer in God, but he was an individual who had matured and reached a peak of knowing right from wrong. Joseph always made sound decisions that could not be faulted by anyone at any time. This is a level of spiritual maturity every believer who knows the Lord prays to God to attain. In 1 Peter 3:16, Peter points out the importance of good conscience when making a decision about any matter. When you do not follow the ways of the world, which are ungodly and non-Christian, many in society may not agree with you. Regardless, you, as a believer, must continue to do what Christ would do. In time those who have spoken against you will come to understand why you have decided to live a Christ-centered life.

RISING ABOVE PUBLIC PERSPECTIVES
OR POSITIONS TO ISSUES

Matthew 1:19; 16:23; Job 2:9–10; James 5:10–11; 2
Samuel 6:20–21; Acts 4:19; 5:29

"Not willing to make her a public example" (Matthew 1:19), Joseph, as a believer in God, was different from the people who lived during his time. His approach to family matters was different from those who did not know the Lord. In Ephesians 4:22–24, the Bible declares that being believers means that we are not of the world because we have put off the old self and have put on Christ. We are now renewed in the spirit and walk in righteousness and true holiness. The above verses clearly explain how genuine believers in Christ are different from nonbelievers. Nonbelievers seek civil divorce as the answer to infidelity in a marriage. True believers seek God's help in overcoming unfaithfulness in their marriage. Their approach to infidelity may always be questioned by unbelievers, but in the sight of God, it is the best position His sons and daughters can take.

RELYING ON POSITIONS THAT
PROTECT YOUR PARTNER

Matthew 1:19–20; Malachi 2:16; John 8:4–8; Romans
15:1–2; Colossians 3:12–15; 1 Corinthians 10:24, 33;
Philippians 2:4–5

"Then Joseph her husband, being a just man, and not willing to make
her a publick example, was minded to put her away privily" (Matthew
1:19–20). Joseph was a real believer in God and a mature man of God,
one we can emulate today in our relationships with our spouses. Joseph
was not excited or happy with what he thought his wife had done before
their coming together as husband and wife. Rather, he was pained, but he
decided to keep it to himself and sought an acceptable way to handle this
matter that would not hurt the woman he wanted to have as his wife. In
Colossians 3:12–15, the Bible states that we should

> put on therefore, as the elect of God, holy and beloved,
> bowels of mercies, kindness, humbleness of mind,
> meekness, longsuffering; forbearing one another, and
> forgiving one another, if any man have a quarrel against
> any: even as Christ forgave you, so also do ye. And above
> all these things put on charity, which is the bond of
> perfectness. And let the peace of God rule in your hearts,
> to the which also ye are called in one body; and be ye
> thankful.

Joseph's love for Mary is obvious in his not subjecting her to public
shame. Also, we understand that Joseph was mindful of what Mary might
be thinking during this difficult time in her life. Indeed, Joseph had the
mind of Christ that genuine believers who are walking with God today
must possess.

Theme

THE INDISPENSABILITY OF JESUS IN THE LIFE OF ANY PERSON ON EARTH

Text(s): Matthew 1:21–23

Lesson Introduction: After the fall of Adam and Eve, the total redemption of humanity was made possible by God, through the provision of God's sacrificial lamb. Christ, as the sacrificial lamb, offers salvation to those who come to God through Him. Christ provides protection to those who rely on Him on earth. He also provides power to live life victoriously by dominating and overcoming the wicked ones. According to the book of Genesis (3:14–15), the seed of Satan and the seed of the woman will continually be in conflict. This translates to Satan and the Lord waging a spiritual fight between themselves and, by extension, Satan's followers and the people of God opposing each other. Eventually, Jesus would suffer death, but He would deal a final blow to Satan by His resurrection. Jesus's resurrection from death is God's triumph over Satan and all his activities, principalities, and powers (Colossians 2:15).

BREAKDOWN OF THE STUDY

1. The prophecy about Jesus
2. The potency behind Jesus's name
3. The purpose of Jesus

THE PROPHECY ABOUT JESUS

> Matthew 1:21; Isaiah 7:14; 9:6–7; Zechariah 9:9; Matthew
> 21:4–10; Psalm 41:9; John 13:18; Matthew 26:14–16;
> Daniel 9:26; Matthew 27:50

The angel of the Lord prophesied that Mary would bring forth a son and that His name would be called Jesus (Matthew 1:21). The prophetic revelation in the New Testament about the birth of Christ is not the only confirmation of His coming to the world through Mary. In the Old Testament, the prophet Isaiah saw Christ coming into the world through a virgin woman called Mary (Isaiah 7:14). Furthermore, in Isaiah 9:6–7, Christ is described as wonderful, counselor, the mighty God, the everlasting father, and the prince of peace. It is also noted that "of the increase of his government and peace there shall be no end."

Other prophecies associated with the coming of Christ can be found in other places in the scriptures. For example, we have information about Christ riding on a donkey's colt (Zechariah 9:9); that Christ would be betrayed by a friend (Psalm 41:9); that the betrayal would be for thirty pieces of silver (Zechariah 11:12); that the Messiah would die a sacrificial death for us (Daniel 9:26; Isaiah 53:8); that Christ would die with a criminal but His burial would be with the wealthy (Isaiah 53:9); that Christ would rise from the dead (Psalm 16:8; Isaiah 53:10); that Christ would say certain words on the cross; that He would be mocked; and that people would gamble for His clothes (Psalm 22:1, 8, 18).

THE POTENCY BEHIND JESUS'S NAME

> Matthew 1:21; Revelation 20:1–3; Hebrews 7:25; John
> 14:12; 11:32–44

Jesus is presented to us as the one to save people from their sins (Matthew 1:21). From Genesis to Revelation, He is the only one the Bible reveals to us as a savior. The word "save," as it is used in Matthew 1:21, is synonymous with power—meaning that Jesus has the power to remit or forgive sins because of His true acceptance and recognition by His heavenly Father.

Jesus Himself said that all power has been given to Him in heaven and in earth (Matthew 28:18). This indicates that Jesus has the backing of God to do whatever He wants to do in heaven and in earth without anyone, even Satan, opposing Him (Revelation 20:1–3).

Christ manifested His power over death when He brought Lazarus back to life four days after he had died. Jesus told Martha that her brother would rise again—meaning that at any minute, He, Jesus Christ, would bring Lazarus back to life (John 11:32–44). In John 14:12, Jesus declares that anyone who believes in Him will do all He has done and even do greater than Him because He goes to the Father. In other words, Jesus gives power to those who believe in Him to bring people back to life. Peter and Paul, the disciples of Jesus, brought the dead ones back to life in the name of Jesus. And there are people in our contemporary time whom God uses to manifest power in the name of Jesus.

THE PURPOSE OF JESUS

> Matthew 1:22–23; 28:20; Isaiah 7:14; Psalm 46:11; 2 Timothy 4:17; Acts 18:9–10

The angel of the Lord told Joseph to name Mary's child Jesus. The angel also referred to the child as "Emmanuel," meaning "God with us" (Matthew 1:23). The only people who are bold enough to say that God is with them are those who believe Him and obey His commandments (Matthew 28:20). Satan is the god of this world, as evidenced by the way people continue to live their lives contrary to God's Word (2 Corinthians 4:4). Satan continues to influence activities on earth. In order to stay above and beyond the reach of Satan, it is necessary to have Jesus (Emmanuel) with us. In Philippians 2:10, we are told that at the mention of Jesus's name, every knee must bow. This implies that, when we call upon Jesus, all the works of the devil must give way.

Theme

A GLORIOUS LIFE, IMPENDING CHALLENGES AND VICTORY OF GOD FOR APPROVED MINISTERS

Text(s): Matthew 2:1–20

Lesson Introduction: Every approved servant of God experiences serious threats from the adversary. It is easy to say that the kingdom of God faces opposition from the kingdom of darkness on earth. In other words, darkness goes after light in the world, in an attempt to frustrate the plans of God for humankind.

In Genesis 3:15, the Lord reveals the enmity that will continue between Satan's seed and the seed of the woman (Jesus). This revelation signals the constant war between the kingdom of darkness and the kingdom of light. He will continue to fight those who have made a decision to do God's will, by going against them and frustrating all of their plans. The New Testament records that Jesus, the promised one, faced the threat of death from the moment that Herod learned that he was the newborn king of the Jews. However, because God had divinely chosen and approved Jesus, Jesus survived the threat of death. Rather, Herod the aggressor was taken down by God.

BREAKDOWN OF THE STUDY

1. Adulation for the Savior
2. Adversity of the Savior
3. Assistance for the Savior

ADULATION FOR THE SAVIOR

> Matthew 2:1–2; 9–11; Luke 2:8–20; 25–30; 36–38;
> Zechariah 9:9; Hebrews 1:6; John 12:13; Psalm 45:11

Jesus, the promised one of God, was foretold of by the prophets, as the chosen one to save the people. God revealed Jesus's birth to the wise men, who, upon spotting the star in the east, came all the way from their country to Jerusalem to worship Him (Matthew 2:1–2). In the book of Luke (2:18–20), the angel of the Lord shared the news of the birth of Jesus with the shepherds in the fields. Those shepherds heard about the birth of Christ and visited Jerusalem and shared the news with those people they encountered along their way. Verses 25–33 of the same chapter reveal the testimony of Simeon, a resident of Jerusalem. Simeon was a godly man who had devoted his life to God. As a result of the love that Simeon had for God, the Holy Ghost revealed to him that he would not see death until he had witnessed the birth of Christ. All of those who understood the mission of Jesus in the world showed Him reverent admiration. Those who believe in Jesus today still show adulation for Christ because they know how significant He is in their lives.

ADVERSITY OF THE SAVIOR

> Matthew 2:2–8, 13, 16; Genesis 3:15; Exodus 1:16; 2:1–3;
> Acts 7:57–59; 2 Timothy 3:12

The Word of God in Genesis 3:15, which declares that God would "put enmity between thy seed and her seed," came to fulfillment when Herod, as the messenger of Satan, became an enemy and a serious threat to the newborn Christ child. Herod received the news of the birth of Jesus who was to be the king of the Jews, the governor and the one who should rule His people. Herod was envious and ordered the destruction of the child (Matthew 2:2–6, 8, 13, 16). The Bible helps us to see others like Jesus, who were called to serve God and lead the people of their time to God, experiencing anguish and adversity from the enemies of their God. For example, Jeremiah, Daniel, Shadrach, Meshach, Abednego, and Joseph witnessed adversity in their lives for their devotion to the one true God. In 2 Timothy 3:12, the Bible states that "all that will live godly in Christ Jesus shall suffer persecution." This verse of the scripture tells us that anyone who purposes to live a distinguished life in Jesus will face adversity similar to that which Jesus faced. Many disciples of Christ and church leaders, like Stephen, faced persecution and death for their identification with Jesus.

ASSISTANCE FOR THE SAVIOR

Matthew 2:13, 15, 19–20; 28:20; 2 Timothy 4:17; Jeremiah 15:20–21; Joshua 1:9; Judges 2:18; Isaiah 8:10; Acts 12:11; 5:19

God was involved directly or indirectly in Herod's death, because Herod was doing everything possible to stop the plans of God for Jesus from coming to fulfilment. In Matthew 2:13, 15, 19–20, the angel of the Lord shared the plans of God about doing something with the enemy of Jesus. According to the angel, God would find a way to fend off Herod's threat in order for Christ to continue the mission God had called Him to do in this world. In Acts 18:9–10, the Lord spoke to Paul telling him not to worry about his life because God would see that nobody succeeded in hurting him. Other people in the Bible have been assured of maximum protection from their enemies; for example: Jeremiah, Abraham, Isaac, and Joshua. Furthermore, people in our own time have the backing of God against all the plans of the devil for their lives.

THE DISCIPLINED LIFE
AND EFFECTIVE MINISTRY
OF JOHN THE BAPTIST

Text(s): Matthew 3:1–9; Malachi 4:5–6

Lesson Introduction: The prophecy in the book of Malachi, chapter 4, verses 5–6, about the coming of John the Baptist in the likeness of Elijah came into fulfillment after four hundred years. That means that the voice of inspiration was silent for four centuries (the interval between the Old Testament and the New Testament), until the birth of John the Baptist was announced to Zechariah (Luke 1:13). During those four centuries, it was imperative for the people to remember and abide by the Law of Moses (Malachi 4:4), because God did not send prophets to the nations to keep calling them back to Himself. Unfortunately, the people who lived during that period interpreted the Law of Moses as they wanted, and everyone did what was right in his own eyes (Judges 21:25). However, the arrival of John the Baptist brought a great revival and a thorough clarification of the genuine meaning and understanding of *repentance.*

BREAKDOWN OF THE STUDY

1. Personal Faithfulness to Mandate
2. Preaching to the Fallen Man
3. Pursuit of the Fruits of Repentance

PERSONAL FAITHFULNESS TO MANDATE

Matthew 3:1–2, 4; Philippians 1:20–21; Romans 8:35–39; Galatians 6:14; Joshua 24:15; John 6:67–68; Psalm 119:106; Acts 11:23

John the Baptist was faithful to the call of God on his life. He demonstrated discipline by not giving himself to sensual and worldly lusts that would derail him from the ministry that God had given him. The mandate given to him was to prepare the way of the Lord and to make his paths straight (Matthew 3:3). His conviction and belief in his unusual assignment fortified him to achieve the impossible during his time.

John the Baptist had no precedent for learning the art of starting a ministry. He alone knew what he needed to do. There was no one to assist him in his ministry. Despite living among people who were indisposed to the laws of God, John the Baptist's faithfulness to his call brought about a spiritual awakening in those to whom he preached.

PREACHING TO THE FALLEN MAN

Matthew 3:1–2, 5–7; 4:17; Acts 2:38; 17:30; Luke 24:47; 15:7; 2 Timothy 2:25–26; Mark 1:14–15

John the Baptist went out to the people preaching the message of repentance. Repentance means a change of mind which results in a change of conduct. In Matthew 3:1, we come across the word *preaching*. John the Baptist put emphasis on preaching repentance to the people who had abandoned and forgotten the ways of the Lord. John the Baptist was focused on teaching repentance and emphasizing what repentance was all about.

In Matthew 4:17, we learn that Jesus Christ continued the work of John the Baptist by preaching repentance to the people. Likewise, other disciples of Christ and Paul, the apostle, recognized that preaching repentance to the fallen man is a mandatory assignment to which all preachers must be faithful. In our own time, preachers have a responsibility to focus on preaching the message of repentance only, and we cannot separate from the foundation laid down by John the Baptist, Jesus Christ, the disciples of Christ, and the apostle Paul.

PURSUIT OF THE FRUITS OF REPENTANCE

Matthew 3:7–10; 21:28–30; Acts 26:20; Ephesians 5:9;
Luke 3:8, 10–14; Jeremiah 36:3; Isaiah 1:16–17

John the Baptist was a fiery preacher, and his uncompromising stance on the Word of God could be seen in his preaching to the religious leaders of his day (Matthew 3:7). John the Baptist was unsparing when it came to the Word of God, for he understood that everyone needed to repent, regardless of their status in society. In his ministry, he wanted those people who came for a baptism by water to have a clear understanding of repentance.

According to John the Baptist, genuine repentance is far more than an intellectual change of mind. Genuine repentance proves itself by the fruits of a changed life. He did not mince words when he shared with the people that those who faked it or pretended to have genuine repentance would be spotted on the day of reckoning (Matthew 3:10). Likewise, Jesus spoke to the people and said, "Except ye repent, ye shall all likewise perish" (Luke 13:3, 5).

Theme

RECOGNIZING AND AVOIDING COMMON THREATS TO THE MINISTRY OF A MAN OF GOD

Text(s): Matthew 4:1–10

Lesson Introduction: As well as a servant and a minister of God on earth, Christ was the Son of God. As God's servant and minister on earth, Christ faced many of the same challenges and threats that some of the Old Testament servants and ministers had encountered. He experienced serious temptations that were meant to destroy the ministry He was sent to fulfill. In Luke 3:23, we learn that when Jesus was around thirty years of age, which was early in his ministry, He was able to overcome the temptations Satan threw at Him by following the Word of God which had been placed on His heart. We observe that, because Jesus had the Word of God in His heart, He was always ready to confront threats to His faith. Jesus did not know that Satan was coming to test Him, but when Satan showed up, Jesus withstood and prevailed over Satan. The lesson that we learn from Jesus's example is that, by taking in the Word of God and digesting it, we will be well armed to face Satan's temptations when they come.

BREAKDOWN OF THE STUDY

1. Avoiding the Practice of Selfishness
2. Avoiding Promotion of Self
3. Avoiding Position Seeking

AVOIDING THE PRACTICE OF SELFISHNESS

Matthew 4:2–4; 2 Corinthians 8:9; 6:10; 11:9; Philippians 1:15; Acts 24:26; 20:35; Hebrews 13:16; Romans 15:1; Matthew 25:34–40; Psalm 41:1–3

Satan observed that Jesus was physically and spiritually spent after fasting for forty days. Therefore, Satan came to Him and challenged Him to turn a stone into bread. As the Son of God, Jesus was capable of turning a stone into bread; however, turning a stone into bread for His own benefit would have been a selfish act, and Jesus chose not to do so. Rather, He was interested in providing bread to nourish other people. Jesus declared to Satan that "man shall not live by bread alone" (Matthew 4:4).

Students of the Bible understand that bread is synonymous to wealth. When the Bible speaks of bread, it refers to money and those things that make life good or wonderful for anyone. Ministers of God can learn from Jesus's example. Though Jesus was poor, He chose to make others rich (2 Corinthians 8:9). Genuine ministers of God must not be covetous or get in the habit of seeking wealth, because doing so will derail their ministries.

AVOIDING PROMOTION OF SELF

Matthew 4:5–7; 1 Samuel 15:30; Philippians 1:17; John 5:44; 12:43

Some ministers of God attempt to demonstrate the power God has given them by performing miracles. They seek personal recognition and popularity. But Jesus was not willing to demonstrate to Satan the power that God had put in His life. From Jesus's point of view, tempting God would have been a careless and sinful use of His power (Matthew 4:5–7). Contrary to the example that Jesus provided, many modern ministers of God attempt to promote themselves by demonstrating their power, even when it is wrong or sinful for them to carry out such acts. True ministers of God understand that, at all times, we need to please God rather than men.

AVOIDING POSITION SEEKING

Matthew 4:8–10; 1 John 2:15–17; Luke 9:46–48; Mark 9:30–35; 10:45; Philippians 2:3; Romans 12:10

Satan offered to place Jesus in a position of power over the whole world and everything in it. Jesus knew, however, that He could not do what Satan suggested and still obey the will of His Father. The example that Jesus gave is clear: ministers of God cannot be in competition with the people of the world in seeking position. If we are to stay true to the call of God upon our lives, those of us who have been called into the ministry must not go about seeking position the way nonbelievers do. John the Beloved counsels serious believers not to love the world, because loving the world indicates we do not love our heavenly Father (1 John 2:15–17). It is unfortunate that in our contemporary world, some ministers of God are seriously seeking the very things that Jesus rejected. To become involved in the worldly rat race is to ignore the important assignment the Lord has called us to do for Him. If you know a minister of God who is consumed with acquiring power and position, you are witnessing someone who has abandoned the ministry that God has called him to fulfill.

PRIORITIZATION THAT YIELDS MAXIMUM GAINS

Text(s): Matthew 4:12–25

Lesson Introduction: Our Lord and Savior, Jesus Christ, demonstrated through His actions how His believers can achieve more for God when we properly understand how we should witness to Him in certain circumstances. Ignorance of Christ's approach to those who would not hearken to His word can place us in danger and cause us to achieve far less for God. The Bible tells us in Proverbs 4:7 that "wisdom is the principal thing; therefore get wisdom: and with all thy getting get understanding." Jesus Christ emphasized that, if the people we are trying hard to evangelize through the gospel of the kingdom of God will not receive us, then we should go to other places (Matthew 10:23). By His words and actions in leaving Nazareth to preach in Galilee, Christ gave an example of how best to react when we are faced with hostility and serious threats to our lives for preaching the gospel. Like Christ, we are better off to leave such hostile environments (cities and countries) and go to other places where God has opened their doors for us. The Word of God makes clear that we need not risk our lives to carry out His ministry.

BREAKDOWN OF THE STUDY

1. Wisdom in Carrying Out the Work of the Ministry
2. Working in Capernaum to compensate for the Change in Ministry's Focus

3. Wonderful Compensation in Capernaum for Changing the Course of His Ministry

WISDOM IN CARRYING OUT THE WORK OF THE MINISTRY

Matthew 4:12; Acts 9:23–25; 17:10–15; 20:1–6; 25:11; 14:5–7; 2 Corinthians 11:32–33; John 7:1–8; Matthew 10:23; Luke 4:43–44

Christ showed wisdom in leaving the city of Nazareth, upon learning about John the Baptist's imprisonment for the sake of preaching the gospel. Jesus knew that the same fate awaited Him. Therefore, He made a prudent decision to leave Nazareth for His own safety. Jesus knew that He could continue His ministry of bringing people to God in other places. Christ realized that God had closed the door of Nazareth to evangelization at that point and that He would do well to carry the gospel message to other places. More importantly, Jesus understood His role in salvation. If He was put in prison or killed, the gospel would not reach the people He was sent into the world to save. Because of Christ's ministry of salvation, His safety meant more than the safety of any other person on earth. Likewise, modern ambassadors of God, who have the significant role of bringing the lost to Christ, are very precious in God's sight. Therefore, those ministers have to be wise and know the Word of God in order to fulfill their ministries.

WORKING IN CAPERNAUM TO COMPENSATE FOR THE CHANGE IN MINISTRY'S FOCUS

Matthew 4:13–16; Mark 1:14; Isaiah 9:1–2; Acts 8:1–5; 11:19

When it became too dangerous for Christ to continue preaching in Nazareth, He decided to go to Capernaum to preach the Word of God. The Bible tells us in Matthew 4:16 that "the people who sat in darkness saw great light and to them which sat in the region and shadow of death light is sprung up." This statement indicates to us that God allowed Jesus

Christ to experience a breakthrough by His ministry in Capernaum. Even in Old Testament times, Isaiah the prophet foretold of Christ going to Capernaum to reach out to the people there about the kingdom of God (Isaiah 9:1–2). The example of Christ in our text reveals to us that God wants us to reach out to other people and not be tied to places where we are not currently experiencing breakthroughs in His work.

WONDERFUL COMPENSATION IN CAPERNAUM FOR CHANGING THE COURSE OF HIS MINISTRY

Matthew 4:17–25; Acts 8:5–6; John 4:3–19, 21–30

No one can argue the success that Jesus Christ experienced in Capernaum. It was during His preaching in Capernaum that Christ first encountered Peter, Andrew, James, and John, who became His disciples. When Jesus Christ departed this world, those four disciples became strong pillars of the church. In addition to selecting His disciples, Christ performed outstanding miracles by "healing all manner of sickness and all manner of disease among the people" (Matthew 4:23). God wants His ministers to accomplish similar successes in our lives. It is absolutely clear that obeying God and His Word will bring huge success to the work we do for Him. We need to serve Him faithfully, until He decides to call us to glory.

AN UNCOMMON DECISION THAT SECURES HEAVEN AND EARTH FOR A SEEKER

Text(s): Matthew 5:1–5

Lesson Introduction: Jesus Christ, in His Sermon on the Mount, was not teaching those who were present how to be saved. Rather, in the passage known as the Beatitudes, He began by telling those people the blessings or happiness to be enjoyed by those who make the effort to encounter God in their spiritual pursuit. Jesus Christ stated that those who seek the Lord as a spiritual power in their lives will find God and that their expectations will not be denied them. According to Jesus Christ, the blessings of God manifest in one's life as a result of seeking those intangible, heavenly approved inward changes of heart and life.

BREAKDOWN OF THE STUDY

1. The Sinner's Spiritual Understanding about His Life
2. The Sinner's Spiritual Understanding about His Life that Leads to Sorrowful State
3. The Saints' Supreme Unparalleled Exploit on Earth

THE SINNER'S SPIRITUAL UNDERSTANDING ABOUT HIS LIFE

Matthew 5:1–3; Acts 16:30; 2:37; Luke 3:10; 5:8; Isaiah 6:5; Job 42:5–6

Jesus Christ spoke about God's blessing on those people who see themselves as poor in the spirit in Matthew 5:1–3. His preaching was not to convict the people who came to listen to His preaching; rather, Christ was informing those present that having an awareness of their spiritual state and seeking the Lord for forgiveness would allow them to enter into the kingdom of heaven. To be "poor in the spirit" means that one is unqualified to stand in the presence of God as a result of being spiritually unclean or low in His sight. However, the awareness of being low in the spirit helps one seek God and rely upon Him to fill that void in one's life. Jesus is saying that desiring God in one's life means a person must first stop sinning, and then seek help from God so as to please Him.

THE SINNER'S SPIRITUAL UNDERSTANDING ABOUT HIS LIFE THAT LEADS TO SORROWFUL STATE

Matthew 5:4; 26:75; 2 Corinthians 7:10; Luke 18:13; 2 Samuel 12:13; Jonah 3:10; 1 Kings 21:27–29; 2 Kings 5:17

There is a connection between verses 3 and 4 of Matthew chapter 5. The poor in spirit in verse 3, who are low in spiritual accomplishment, suddenly become awakened about their spiritual status. This awakening causes one to mourn or cry because he/she has gone very far into doing things that are contrary to the will of God. Mourning or feeling sorrowful for sin has been seen as a genuine form of inward repentance by those who really felt the burden or weight of their sin.

The importance of mourning for one's sin cannot be overemphasized today. It is as a result of genuine mourning that God shows mercy. For example, upon hearing the word of God from Elijah, Ahab mourned for the evil that he had committed against Naboth. The Bible shows that Ahab, who was the king, put sackcloth upon his flesh, fasted, lay in sackcloth, and went softly before God (1 Kings 21:27–29).

THE SAINTS' SUPREME UNPARALLELED EXPLOIT ON EARTH

Matthew 5:5; Numbers 12:3, 7; Psalm 37:11; Colossians 3:12; Titus 3:2

Those who have obtained mercy from the Lord for their sins become meek. In other words, those who have been pardoned for living their lives without God become meek and concentrate their entire lives on doing the will of God and pleasing Him. In Matthew 5:5, Jesus Christ said, "Blessed are the meek: for they shall inherit the earth." Meekness is a virtue that a true Christian will manifest as an outcome of consistently working with God. We cannot profess to know the Lord or claim to walk with Him if meekness is not a virtue we practice in our lives. In Numbers 12, Verses 3 and 7, the Bible tells us that Moses was a meek man who was faithful about doing the things of God. The approach of Moses reveals to us that meekness, faithfulness, and diligence are qualities to be sought after in the life of anyone who knows the Lord intimately. Finally, those who are meek will inherit the earth by their exploits in bringing people to Christ and multiplying the kingdom of God on earth.

APPROVED TESTS FOR NEW SPIRITUAL LIFE AND FOR THE MATURED IN CHRIST

Text(s): Matthew 5:1–12

Lesson Introduction: There is no crown without the cross. The crown is a reward from God, and the cross is a place of shame, ridicule, suffering, and pain. This means that before believers in Christ will be privileged to receive the blessings of earth and heaven, they must be prepared to face challenges and persecutions for their devotion to God. The Bible declares in 2 Timothy 3:12, that "all that will live godly in Christ Jesus shall suffer persecution." It is the believers' victory over the enemies of their new faith that will yield the crown of glory.

BREAKDOWN OF THE STUDY

1. Counsel to Obey the Word of Christ
2. Carry Out the Works that Christ Counseled
3. Constant Opposition to the Works that Christ Counseled

COUNSEL TO OBEY THE WORD OF CHRIST

Matthew 5:1–5; John 6:63, 68; 12:49–50; Psalm 119:93; 19:7–10; Deuteronomy 32:46-47; 1 Thessalonians 2:13; Romans 2:25

Jesus Christ taught the multitudes of people who came to listen to Him to think of the blessings that accrue to those who heed His words. The Word of Christ for those people was in three phases. First, people are to consider the blessing attached to recognizing and knowing where they are spiritually. In other words, they are poor in the spirit, and they must not deceive themselves by declaring they are rich (Matthew 5:3). Second, Christ admonished His listeners that, once they accept that they are poor in spirit, they must mourn by weeping or crying for how they have lived their lives without being rich toward God (Matthew 5:4). Lastly, Christ counseled that there is a blessing for being meek in this world (Matthew 5:5). Christ's counsel was not just for the people of His time but is very important counsel for anyone who seeks the blessings of God in their lives before departing this world.

CARRY OUT THE WORKS THAT CHRIST COUNSELED

> Matthew 5:6–9; 7:24; 28:20; Romans 2:13; Luke 11:28; Philippians 4:8; 1 John 2:3; 3:7; 3 John 1:11; Revelation 22:7

Jesus Christ promises salvation to everyone who comes to know God through Him. He counsels His hearers to have their own spiritual lives in order by carrying out works that show they are true followers of Christ.

In Matthew 5:6–9, Christ emphasizes four phases: First, His hearers have to hunger and thirst after righteousness. His hearers are to continue to pray and fast for God's righteousness to manifest in their lives. Second, Christ demands that His hearers begin to show mercy to others—not just as a one-time undertaking but as a continuous experience throughout their lives (Matthew 5:7).

Third, Christ teaches that His hearers need to work on themselves by asking God to purify their hearts in order for them to be holy (Matthew 5:8). Christ's emphasis on purity of heart or sanctification of heart cannot be overemphasized. In the book of Romans (8:29), the Word of God for believers is to always conform to the image of Christ which consists of righteousness and true holiness. In addition, purity of heart is both the end of our election and the goal of our redemption (Ephesians 4:24, 1:4; Titus 2:14).

Fourth, Christ teaches that those who are rich in spiritual things will become peacemakers on earth. People who see them will easily recognize that they indeed belong to Christ (Matthew 5:9).

CONSTANT OPPOSITION TO THE WORKS THAT CHRIST COUNSELED

> Matthew 5:10–12; 10:22; 24:9; James 1:12; Revelation 2:10; 1 John 3:13; John 17:14; 2 Corinthians 4:11; Acts 9:16

Walking righteously and following Jesus Christ in a world that is full of wickedness will not bode well for those who, by the help of God, have discovered they are poor in the spirit. Without a shadow of a doubt, Jesus Christ knows that those who purpose to practice what He teaches will constantly face persecution from those who oppose that way. Christ admonishes those believers, regardless of harassment and opposition, to remain steadfast in walking righteously, because the blessings of God will come upon them. In addition, Christ reminds those who choose to do His will that other great men of God have also faced persecution from the enemy of righteousness. Therefore, those people who are listening to Him should rejoice in suffering at the hands of those people and be exceedingly glad because of the reward that awaits them in heaven.

Theme

DESCRIPTIONS OF A CHRISTIAN THAT HELP TO AVOID BACKSLIDING

Text(s): Matthew 5:13–16

Lesson Introduction: In Matthew 5:1–5, Jesus Christ opens His Sermon on the Mount in which he challenges the gathered multitudes to work on their spiritual lives. He goes on to tell the people to demonstrate their understanding of God by their works. In Matthew 5:13–16, Jesus Christ compares those who have changed their lives to do the will of God to salt and light. Jesus Christ uses these metaphors to emphasize to His believers how indispensable they are in this world. Because of sin, the world can be a dark and bitter place. Believers are the ones called to make this world a better place. At the same time, Jesus Christ points out that when Christians backslide in their faith, they cease to be salt and light for the world.

BREAKDOWN OF THE STUDY

1. Backsliders in the Spirit
2. Believers as Salt
3. Believers as Light

BACKSLIDERS IN THE SPIRIT

> Matthew 5:13; Hebrews 6:4–6; 2 Peter 2:15, 20–21; 2
> Timothy 4:10; Philippians 2:21; Luke 17:32

Backsliding is turning away from the Lord after one has repented and made a conscious decision to follow the Lord. Backsliding leads a believer to abandon the newfound faith and return to his/her evil ways.

In Matthew 5:1–5, Christ taught the people of the need to know where they stand spiritually. He then shared with the people that just as salt can lose its savor (taste), they could forfeit their salvation by losing their spirituality (Matthew 5:13). A person who accepts Christ becomes the "salt of the earth." But a believer who backslides is now a sinner, and his/her actions and works are no different than those who do not know the Lord. Christ's admonition about backsliding should inspire those who call themselves Christians to carefully monitor their spiritual lives on a regular basis, lest they cease to know and follow Christ.

BELIEVERS AS SALT

> Matthew 5:13; 12:34–35; Colossians 4:6; Mark 9:50;
> Leviticus 2:13; Luke 4:22; Ephesians 4:29; Proverbs 15:4,
> 7; Psalm 71:23–24

Jesus Christ used the metaphor of *salt* to describe the hearers and doers of His word. Christ understands that salt is very useful in this life. Some of salt's benefits are that it can be used to add flavor to food, act as a preservative, heal wounds, and melt ice. Christians are salt, and being salt means their positive presence must be felt anywhere they are. Their presence prevents corruption in their communities, helping people to be free from fear and at peace. Therefore, Christians must not be found making trouble or causing commotions, lest they appear as salt that has lost its beneficial properties. Believers who understand their role as "the salt of the earth" will strive to be the kind of salt described by Christ.

BELIEVERS AS LIGHT

Matthew 5:14–16; Philippians 2:15; John 8:12; 12:36; 1
Thessalonians 5:5; Ephesians 5:8–14; 2 Corinthians 6:14

Christ also uses a metaphor when He compares believers to *light*. Jesus sees His believers as lights in the world. Without light, people walk in darkness. Christians have a mission to be light for the world. We are to shine forth into the darkness of human depravity.

Christians who are light cannot be hidden because wherever they are, they shine forth. Christ assures His believers that even the smallest light can extinguish darkness. A true believer in Christ will shine and bring positive change to the multitudes of people with whom they interact. Anyone who desires to be called a Christian must be sincere with themselves by answering the simple question: Am I a light to my family, in my neighborhood, and in my workplace? In summary, Christ is saying, "Let your light shine, through a clean life, before the Lord and before the world in which you live."

Theme

OBEDIENCE TO THE AUTHORITY OF THE SCRIPTURES

Text(s): Matthew 5:17–20

Lesson Introduction: The Bible, in its entirety, is the Word of God. It is a costly mistake to reject the infallibility of the Word (the Bible). In Romans 15:4, the Bible states that "whatsoever things were written aforetime were written for our learning, that we through patience and comfort of the scriptures might have hope." This verse reinforces the authority of the Old Testament and emphasizes the importance of learning from it, for our profitability. We cannot accept the New Testament and ignore the teachings in the Old Testament. Both the Old and the New Testaments point believers to lead lives that are both inwardly and outwardly righteous.

BREAKDOWN OF THE STUDY

1. Completeness of the Bible
2. Comparison of Bible Teachers
3. The Core Bible Teaching

COMPLETENESS OF THE BIBLE

Matthew 5:17–18; Psalm 19:7; 2 Timothy 3:15–17; Joshua 1:8; Romans 7:22; Proverbs 30:5

Having laid the foundation of His message in the summary statements of the Beatitudes, Jesus Christ now proceeds to show the superiority of that message to that of the Law of Moses. He makes it clear that He did not come to destroy the Old Testament law. The New Testament gospel is neither contrary to nor contradictory of the Old Testament law; rather, it is the ultimate fulfillment of the spiritual intention of the law.

Although the law had been reduced to legalism by the Pharisees, Jesus now took the law beyond mere outward observance to the inner spiritual intention of God. Jesus Christ came to fulfill the law and its fullest implications. In His earthly life, Jesus accomplished this by meeting the strictest demands of the law and going beyond its mere outward requirements. Matthew 5:18 begins with Jesus using the phrase *Verily I say unto you*. This is a unique form used by Jesus throughout the Bible to draw attention to the authority of His message. *Verily* means truly, certainly, or amen. It is used as a designation of authoritative teaching. Jesus Christ, considering the Old and the New Testaments, declares that heaven and earth will pass away, but the law (the Bible) will not pass away until all is fulfilled. This informs us that the Bible, the law of God, is perfect and complete, and we cannot pick and choose what we want to hear and believe.

COMPARISON OF BIBLE TEACHERS

> Matthew 5:19; Malachi 2:8–9; James 2:10–11; Psalm 119:6; 2 Corinthians 4:2; Acts 20:27; Romans 16:17–18; Philippians 1:15–18

In Matthew 5:19, Jesus Christ compares two Bible teachers. Both teachers are capable of teaching the Word of God; however, the teachers practice and obey the Word of God differently in their lives, and they teach the Word of God differently. Therefore, Jesus Christ declares different outcomes for the two teachers. The first Bible teacher compromises the Word by not obeying it in its totality in his life and teaches the Word of God incompletely to his hearers. This person would receive less commendation and would be called least in the kingdom of God. The second Bible teacher, who faithfully lives out the Word in his life and teaches the complete and thorough Word of

God to his hearers, would be called great in the kingdom of God. Christ's comparison informs us that we cannot cherry-pick the Word of God. Rather, the Word of God must be obeyed in its entirety.

THE CORE BIBLE TEACHING

> Matthew 5:8–9, 20; 1 Timothy 6:11; Hebrews 12:14; 2 Corinthians 7:1; 1 Thessalonians 4:7; 1 Peter 1:15–16; 2 Peter 3:11, 14

Jesus Christ's teaching is that the law goes far beyond formalism. Unlike the scribes and Pharisees, Christ wants His hearers to have an inward experience of righteousness that will take them to heaven. The understanding of righteousness the scribes and Pharisees had was expressed externally by what they ate and how they prayed and in their physical appearance. But Jesus Christ declares to His hearers that their righteousness must exceed that demonstrated by the scribes and Pharisees. While it is good to pursue outward righteousness as the scribes and Pharisees did, it is essential for true believers to exceed the formalities of the law by internalizing its spirit. The core teaching in both the Old and New Testaments is that true believers must live a righteous life. In other parts of the Bible, Christ, the prophets, and Christ's disciples express the idea of righteousness using the synonyms *perfection*, *holiness*, *purity*, and *godliness*.

Theme

THE WEIGHTY COMMANDS THAT SEPARATE CHRISTIANS FROM FORMALISTIC RELIGION

Text(s): Matthew 5:21–26

Lesson Introduction: Believers who follow the teachings of Christ, as outlined in Matthew 5, will achieve a complete change of heart. Those who have come in contact with Christ's teachings on how to live a spiritual life should live lives that are completely different from other religious practitioners in the world. The scribes and Pharisees focused on external actions and not on living a spiritual life. However, Christ's teachings call His followers to live lives that distinguish them from non-practitioners of their faith. Following His instructions changes the lives of believers, both inwardly and outwardly. Christ referred to His followers becoming the salt and light of the world as a result of their conduct among the people around them.

BREAKDOWN OF THE STUDY

1. Crime Charge Not Central to Christ's Teachings
2. Changes that Conform to Christ's Teachings
3. Consistency in Carrying Out Christ's Teachings

CRIME CHARGE NOT CENTRAL
TO CHRIST'S TEACHINGS

> Matthew 5:21, 38; Exodus 20:13; Numbers 35:30–34; 1
> Kings 2:5–6; Luke 19:8

In Matthew 5:21, Jesus Christ quotes Exodus 20:13, which says "Thou shalt not kill," and continues to cite people's understanding that whoever kills is "in danger of the judgment." The reference to killing is clearly understood in its context in both the Old and New Testaments as referring to an act of murder. All of the religions in the world oppose murder in all forms, and the community at large understands the consequence of wrongfully taking other people's lives. Christ's message on the Mount is to denounce the religious scribes and Pharisees on formalism religion. The Pharisees and the scribes believe that obeying the law of an "eye for an eye" does portray anyone as doing God's will or as a godly person. However, Christ teaches that emphasizing outward righteousness (meting out judgment to the offender), as the scribes and Pharisees do, without curbing the root cause of murder in the offender is not *transformational* and does not qualify one to be called a true follower of God or a heaven seeker.

CHANGES THAT CONFORM TO
CHRIST'S TEACHINGS

> Matthew 5:22–23; 1 John 3:14–15; James 3:2; Ephesians
> 4:26–27, 31–32; 1 Peter 3:9; 2:23; Romans 12:10; Titus
> 3:2; 1 Thessalonians 4:6

Christ's standard or expectation for those who know and walk with Him is very high. The Lord's followers should have experienced a change of heart, which translates to possessing the godly virtues of love, joy, peace, longsuffering, endurance, meekness, and temperance. Therefore, true believers should refrain from demonstrating anger and using derogatory words against people.

According to Jesus Christ, believers who harbor anger towards their fellow brothers, for no apparent reason, will face heavenly judgment. He also says who demeans a brother by calling him *raca*, an insulting term meaning "vain or empty head," will face the heavenly council. In addition, believers who use the word *fools* to describe their fellow human beings will be in danger of hellfire (Matthew 5:22–23).

Christ helps us see that a true believer, one who is desperate to please the Lord and get to heaven, will guard his heart and carefully monitor his speech on a daily basis. On the contrary, a false believer will resort to the use of foul language and cursing whenever he wants. False believers will face God's judgment and are in danger of spending eternity in hellfire.

CONSISTENCY IN CARRYING OUT CHRIST'S TEACHINGS

> Matthew 5:24–26; Acts 23:1–5; 24:16; James 5:16; Romans 12:17–18; 1 Peter 3:7–8; Job 42:8

Christ's teachings are about being truly righteous and following the spirit of the law, not just the letter of the law as the scribes and the Pharisees did. The apostle Paul describes this righteousness in Acts 24:16, when he says, "And herein do I exercise myself, to have always a conscience void of offence toward God, and toward men." Paul is saying that he strives to avoid offending God and mankind.

For Christians, the goal is to be perfect and offense-less. However, when Christians observe that they have offended God or man, they must apologize for their actions and provide restitution where possible. In Matthew 5:24–26, Christ commands Christians to seek peace with those they have offended before bringing their tithes and offerings to the house of God. Christ counsels us to keep peace with others so that we can confidently stand before Him as righteous believers.

Theme

THE GODLY VIRTUES ACTIVE IN BELIEVERS IN CHRIST

Text(s): Matthew 5:21–22, 27–28, 31–32

Lesson Introduction: Christ's Sermon on the Mount as related in Matthew, chapters 5-7, can be briefly summarized: to move from being a sinner to a saint, one must strive to "be ye therefore perfect, even as your Father which is in heaven is perfect" (Matthew 5:48). His teachings create an awareness of the need to make a conscious decision to do God's will. Also, believers are encouraged to demonstrate their brand-new spiritual life by acting as "salt" and "light" in the world. And then, Christ shares with His hearers that He opposes the teachings of the scribes and Pharisees, because of their emphasis on external righteousness. In other words, the scribes and Pharisees, while they follow the letter of the law, fail to allow the laws of God to permeate their own lives so as to create desirable changes in their society. A quick recap of Matthew 5 is that Christ teaches that those who know and follow Him must abide by His teachings in their conduct in all circumstances.

BREAKDOWN OF THE STUDY

1. Delightful Words Superior to Abhorrence and Murder
2. Defeat over Wayward Heart Superior to Sin of Adultery and Lust
3. Demonstration of Warmth to Your Spouse is Superior to Divorce

DELIGHTFUL WORDS SUPERIOR TO ABHORRENCE AND MURDER

Matthew 5:21–22, 33–36, 38, 43–44; Colossians 4:6; Ephesians 4:29; Psalm 34:13; Isaiah 50:4; 1 Samuel 25:23–32

Christ condemns the teachings of the scribes and the Pharisees because the religious leaders fail to deal with the fundamental issues. Murder starts in the heart with the feeling of abhorrence. The feeling may be subtle at first but with time, if not curbed or dealt with, reaches an intensity that may lead to murder. The root causes of murder are anger, hatred, envy, unpleasant remarks, and careless words being used toward others. Just as Christ condemns murder, He likewise condemns anger, hatred, and unpleasant remarks from people who call themselves His true followers. Christ's indirect message to His hearers is to charge them to be in control of their spiritual lives at all times. In other words, true Christians who make God the central focus in their daily lives will speak delightful words in all circumstances, regardless of what they are going through.

DEFEAT OVER WAYWARD HEART SUPERIOR TO SIN OF ADULTERY AND LUST

Matthew 5:27–28; 15:19; James 1:14–15; Mark 7:21–23; Proverbs 4:23; 13:3; Psalm 139:23–24

The scribes and the Pharisees stick with the commandment given in the Old Testament not to commit adultery (Exodus 20:14). According to the scribes and the Pharisees, their obligation is to just abide by the literal interpretation of the law. But Christ, in His teaching on the Mount, explains to His hearers that the teaching on adultery is deeper than what is taught by the religious leaders.

Christ gives a weightier command than what the law states. Christ teaches that "whosoever looketh on a woman to lust after her hath committed adultery with her already in his heart" (Matthew 5:28). This interpretation indicates that the lustful look is the expression of a heart that says in essence, I would if I could. The act would follow if the opportunity were to occur. Christ states that, in order not to be condemned as adulterers and adulteresses, His followers need to have victory over waywardness in their hearts on a daily basis.

DEMONSTRATION OF WARMTH TO YOUR SPOUSE IS SUPERIOR TO DIVORCE

> Matthew 5:31–32, 39, 41–48; 1 Corinthians 7:15; Ephesians 5:1; 2 Corinthians 2:7; 4:31; Colossians 3:12–13; 1 Peter 3:8–9

"It hath been said" is a reference to the Old Testament commandment of the Mosaic regulation (Deuteronomy 24:1). The normal custom of the ancient Near East was for a man to verbally divorce his wife. The Arab custom was to say "I divorce you" three times, whereupon the divorce was concluded, without any legal protection of any kind to the wife. In contrast, the ancient law of Israel insisted on a writing of divorcement or a certificate of divorce. This written statement gave legal protection to both the wife and the husband. Christ's words in Matthew 5:32 are in direct contrast to both of these customs. Christ states that divorce is not to be practiced by His followers except in the case of fornication. Jesus Christ said that a man can put away his wife only for the sin of fornication and not for other sins. Furthermore, He says that, if the wife is divorced for any other reason and another man marries her, that man commits adultery. Rather than pursuing divorce even for fornication, Christ indirectly teaches His believers to show warmth to their spouses instead of putting them away for the sin of the flesh.

Theme

CHRIST'S PERSPECTIVE ON ACCEPTABLE SERVICE BEFORE GOD

Text(s): Matthew 6:1–18

Lesson Introduction: Christ was systematic in His approach to teaching the multitudes of people who came to listen to Him. Paying attention to His teaching in Matthew chapter 5, one observes that Christ started with the fundamentals: 1) coming to know the Lord in the Spirit; 2) walking as salt and light in the world; and 3) growing in grace to perfection in the Lord. Achieving these objectives qualifies believers to approach God in their service to Him.

Christ unequivocally denounced the ways of the *hypocrites* in their service to God, because He saw their service as being rendered to impress men and not to glorify God. In Matthew chapter 6, therefore, Christ taught His hearers the acceptable ways that will reach God and get His attention in their lives. The types of service Christ taught His hearers must all be observed in *secret*, without people knowing about them.

BREAKDOWN OF THE STUDY

1. Service through Giving Alms in Secret
2. Service through Praying in Secret
3. Service through Fasting in Secret

SERVICE THROUGH GIVING ALMS IN SECRET

> Matthew 6:1–4; Acts 10:2–4, 31; 9:36; Luke 7:4–5;
> Hebrews 6:10

The alms that Jesus speaks about refer to charitable contributions made to those in need. In Matthew 6:2, Christ speaks of the hypocrites who can be found in the synagogues and in the streets. Such hypocrites give their alms not out of love for their needy fellow humans but out of a prideful desire for people to see them and praise them. However, Christ instructs believers not to be like the hypocrites but to give alms in secret. He assures His believers that God, who sees in the secret, will bless such people in the open. It cannot be overemphasized that this teaching of Christ has to be learned and practiced by true believers, because there is a possibility that believers will come to the aid of the needy only in anticipation of getting attention from the public.

SERVICE THROUGH PRAYING IN SECRET

> Matthew 6:5–15; 14:23; 26:36–39; 2 Kings 4:33; Isaiah
> 26:20; Acts 9:40; 10:9, 30; Genesis 32:24–29; Ezra 9:5–6;
> Daniel 6:10; Luke 1:12–13; 2 Chronicles 32:24

Christ denounced the hypocrite's way of offering prayers, both in the synagogues and in the streets. Christ passionately declared that those who present themselves as pious in the eyes of men "love" to pray in the synagogue and in the streets mainly to be seen and acknowledged by the public. In other words, Christ declared that those who covet the approval of men will never get the approval of God.

If God's faithful believers want God to answer their prayers, they must learn to practice praying as God directs, in secret. The due diligence to be followed by believers in Christ is to enter into one's closet, shut the door, and offer sincere prayers to God from one's heart. When one prays, one must trust that God cares for him and hears his prayer. Moreover, Jesus instructed, "When ye pray, use not vain repetitions, as the heathen do: for they think that they shall be heard for their much speaking" (Matthew 6:7).

SERVICE THROUGH FASTING IN SECRET

Matthew 6:16–18; Daniel 10:2–3; 9:20–21; 2 Samuel
12:20; Acts 10:30

Christ's teaching on acceptable fasting is different from what is being
practiced by many in society today. Some religions and some churches
announce their periods of fasting, which allows people to observe and
acknowledge their good deeds during those periods. However, Christ's
teaching addresses individuals and not what groups of people must do or
obey. Because fasting is a personal, religious observance, those Christians
who choose to fast must not draw attention to themselves by wearing a sad
face or appearing hungry. Rather, a believer in Christ, when he is fasting,
must wear a happy face and be in a joyous mood, so that people will not
recognize he is observing a fast. Those who follow Christ's teaching on
fasting will receive God's attention, and God will answer their prayers. In
the Old Testament, the Bible reveals those individuals who prayed to God
but did not have to worry about their appearance. Those men (David and
Daniel) did not worry about cleansing themselves because they were not
among people who could praise them for being spiritual.

HEAVEN AND THE PURSUIT OF WORLDLY POSSESSIONS BY BELIEVERS

Text(s): Matthew 6:19–24

Lesson Introduction: Christ speaks about worldly possessions as a serious threat to believers who wish to enter the kingdom of heaven. Christ states that believers cannot pursue God and mammon simultaneously but must choose God and renounce mammon (Matthew 6:19). Likewise, John the Beloved counsels believers in Christ in 1 John 2:15–17, "Love not the world, neither the things that are in the world. If any man love the world, the love of the Father is not in him. For all that is in the world, the lust of the flesh, and the lust of the eyes, and the pride of life, is not of the Father, but is of the world. And the world passeth away, and the lust thereof: but he that doeth the will of God abideth forever." These verses confirm the words of Christ that we cannot seek both material wealth and the kingdom of heaven at the same time. Those believers who really want to go to heaven need to close their minds to the riches of the world and seek the kingdom of God.

BREAKDOWN OF THE STUDY

1. Christ's Charge to Make Heaven Our Priority
2. Concentrating Passionately on Heaven
3. Coming to a Crossroads between Desiring Heaven and Desiring Possessions

CHRIST'S CHARGE TO MAKE
HEAVEN OUR PRIORITY

Matthew 6:19–21; Hebrews 11:26; 10:34; 1 Timothy 6:17; Luke 18:22; 12:33; James 2:5

Christ emphasizes the priority of heaven over the world in Matthew 6:19–21. Christ speaks convincingly of the foolishness of any effort to gather possessions in this world. All the riches of this world that one might invest in are subject to depreciation and eventual destruction. Furthermore, all the riches of this world are coveted by thieves who will stop at nothing to steal them to satisfy their own greed. In Matthew 6:19–20, Christ states, "Lay not up for yourself treasures upon earth, where moth and rust doth corrupt, and where thieves break through and steal: But lay up for yourselves treasures in heaven, where neither moth nor rust doth corrupt, and where thieves do not break through nor steal." Due to the transient nature of worldly wealth, Christ urges his believers to make attaining heaven the priority of their lives.

CONCENTRATING PASSIONATELY ON HEAVEN

Matthew 6:22–23; 13:44; 19:21; Luke 14:33; Colossians 1:23; 2 Corinthians 7:1; 1 Thessalonians 4:1; 2 Peter 3:14; Philippians 2:16; 1:26–27; Acts 4:34–37; 2:44–45

Christ teaches His believers to focus on heaven with total concentration and singleness of heart. In Matthew 6:22, Christ employs the following metaphor: "the light of the body is the eye: if therefore thine eye be single, thy whole body shall be full of light." In this verse, Christ reiterates that if His believers are committed to Him and have yielded completely to Him, thoughts about dividing their loyalty between God and worldly possessions will not occur. Furthermore, in Matthew 6:23, Christ implies that those who have heard His word and assume that they are walking in the light of the kingdom of God, but who are still entangled or ensnared by possessions in this world, are still in darkness. Believers who passionately seek heaven by searching for God's undiluted truth and living out that truth in their lives are the ones who are truly living in God's light.

COMING TO A CROSSROADS BETWEEN DESIRING HEAVEN OR DESIRING POSSESSIONS

> Matthew 6:24; 4:8–10; 1 Peter: 2:11; 1 John 2:15–16; James 4:4; 1 Timothy 6:9–10; 1 Samuel 7:3; 2 Timothy 4:10

In 1 Peter 2:11, the apostle beseeches believers as "strangers and pilgrims" on an earthly journey "to abstain from fleshly lusts." Christ's warning about seeking riches on earth, along with Peter's admonition to avoid fleshly lusts, can be a hard pill to swallow for some Christians. Some churches preach a prosperity theology, which promises riches and worldly possessions for their followers. Many of these church members call themselves Christians, and yet they are busy gathering possessions here in the world. Christ's message is very clear about where He stands when it comes to choosing between God and possessions. Christ authoritatively declares that "no man can serve two masters: for either he will hate the one, and love the other; or else he will hold to the one, and despise the other. Ye cannot serve God and mammon" (Matthew 6:24). Christ sees material possessions in this world as a conflict of interest to the goal of pursuing heaven while we are on earth.

GOD, THE CENTER OF FOCUS FOR BELIEVERS ON EARTH

Text(s): Matthew 6:25–34

Lesson Introduction: Christ's central message for believers on earth is to make God their focus. Believers are not to be preoccupied with the mundane things of this world. Rather, our strength must be directed toward knowing God more and more. Believers in Christ are to be remarkably different from nonbelievers or the so-called "pseudo-believers" who have backslidden from their faith in Christ as a result of placing too much emphasis on material accumulation. In Romans 6:16, Paul the apostle declares, "Know ye not, that to whom ye yield yourselves servants to obey, his servants ye are to whom ye obey." This quote reveals there is no middle ground (juggling faith in Christ with laboring to be rich in possessions). Either Christ's believers pursue the kingdom of heaven, as taught to do by Christ, or they believe only in their words but not in their actions.

BREAKDOWN OF THE STUDY

1. Commitment to God as Pilgrims on Our Way to Heaven
2. Confidence in God for Provision on Our Way to Heaven
3. Consciousness of God and Prevailing over Our Challenges on Our Way to Heaven

COMMITMENT TO GOD AS PILGRIMS
ON OUR WAY TO HEAVEN

Matthew 6:19–24; Joshua 24:15; John 6:67–68; Ruth
1:15–16; Psalm 119:106, 111–112; Acts 11:23

The summary of the Lord's words in Matthew 6:19–24 is to inform His
hearers that from the time of their conversion until the time of their death
(if the Lord delays His coming), they must be resolute in their commitment
to the Lord. In addition, Christ emphasizes that possessions, or the
material things of this world, should not be a rival to God's love in our
heart. Christ declares in verse 24, "Ye cannot serve God and mammon."
In other words, believers in God must renounce possessions and stick with
God at all times during their passage in this world. Moreover, for believers,
getting to heaven cannot just be something to be wished for; there must
be a deliberate effort, on a daily basis, to fight all hindrances on the way
to heaven.

CONFIDENCE IN GOD FOR PROVISION
ON OUR WAY TO HEAVEN

Matthew 6:25–32; 7:9; Genesis 1:29–31; Psalm 145:15–
16; 103:13; Luke 12:30; Psalm 84:11; 2 Corinthians 9:8–
11; 1 Timothy 6:17

Christ assures believers of God's divine provision for those who have
confidence in Him. Christ reminds believers of God's unwavering
faithfulness to them by citing as examples the fowls of the air, the lilies of
the field, and the grass that withers and dies. Each of these is less important
than human beings, yet God takes care of them.

Nonbelievers do not believe there is a God somewhere who takes
care of them. Instead, they labor and toil in an attempt to gather wealth,
because they see their goal on earth as to have possessions. However,
Christ's counsel to true believers is this: "Therefore take no thought,
saying, what shall we eat? Or, what shall we drink? Or, wherewithal shall
we be clothed? (For after all these things do the Gentiles seek:) for your

heavenly Father knoweth that ye have need of all these things" (Matthew 6:31–32). Believers must trust in God and not waver.

CONSCIOUSNESS OF GOD AND PREVAILING OVER OUR CHALLENGES ON OUR WAY TO HEAVEN

> Matthew 6:33–34; 5:6; John 6:27; 16:1–3; Acts 14:22; 20:24; 1 Thessalonians 3:3–4; 2:2, 14; 2 Thessalonians 1:4–6; 2 Corinthians 8:1–2

This portion of the Sermon on the Mount is summarized by the statement "Seek ye first the kingdom of God" (Matthew 6:33). The hearers of Christ who have pledged their allegiance to God must continue seeking the kingdom of heaven and its righteousness. The contrast between the spiritual and the material is again emphasized. The believer is to seek first the righteousness that is characteristic of God's kingdom, and then all these (material) things shall be added unto him.

Seeking the kingdom of God involves a continued hunger and thirst after righteousness. We are not only to seek the kingdom of God in the sense that we set our affection on things above, but we must also positively seek holiness in righteousness. The continual seeking here is similar to seeking the face of God. A true believer is never falsely content with what he has in Christ but is continually seeking to know Him better. When our priority is spiritual, He will take care of the material, for where God guides, He provides.

We need not even worry about tomorrow for "sufficient unto the day is the evil thereof" (Matthew 6:34). This means that each day has its own troubles and challenges, to be responsibly handled, without worrying about the hypothetical problems which could arise tomorrow.

Theme

ALLOWING CHRIST'S TEACHINGS TO PROFIT ONE'S LIFE

Text(s): Matthew 7:1–28

Lesson Introduction: The Sermon on the Mount, which began in chapter 5 of the Gospel of Matthew, concludes in chapter 7. In this sermon, Christ has taught a series of lessons about serving God in the Spirit and about how people need to conduct themselves on earth during their pilgrimage to heaven. Christ admonishes His hearers to humble themselves by always seeking God to remove the imperfection in their lives. Christ does not want those who have learned from His teachings and who have changed their lives to become judgmental of others. While it is very easy to condemn people who do not share our religious beliefs and call them fearful names, that is not Christ's way. Rather, the sincere prayer of a serious Christian is that God should uphold him/her to the end.

BREAKDOWN OF THE STUDY

1. Staying Humble before God
2. Seeking and Hoping for God's Gifts
3. Searching for Heaven through the Narrow Way that Leads to God

STAYING HUMBLE BEFORE GOD

> Matthew 7:1–6; 5:5; Psalm 149:4; 25:9; James 3:13; 1:21;
> 1 Peter 3:15; Ephesians 4:2; 2 Timothy 2:25; 1 Timothy
> 6:11; Zephaniah 2:3; Colossians 3:12; Titus 3:2

Christ's message to those who were with Him on the Mount is not to judge other people. Those who have been blessed to hear Christ's message and who have adopted a new way of living may have a tendency to judge other people and see themselves as being superior. Christ knew that those who were with Him on the Mount might assume they were perfect and no longer sinners. They might also assume that the people who were not privileged to hear what they have heard are evil and are going to hell. Instead, Christ beckons to His hearers to always focus inwardly and to work on themselves by removing the beams from their own eyes rather than pointing accusing fingers at others. It cannot be overemphasized that God wants us to remain humble, not to be hypocritical, and to strive each day to please the Lord in our walk with Him.

SEEKING AND HOPING FOR GOD'S GIFTS

> Matthew 7:7–12; 21:22; 1 John 3:22; John 15:7; Psalm
> 145:18–19; James 1:5–6; Jeremiah 33:3; 29:12–13;
> Hebrews 11:6; Luke 18:1; Proverbs 8:17

The Lord teaches His believers to focus on seeking God's gifts in their lives. Continuously seeking spiritual progress in one's life will prompt God to answer our requests. Our heavenly Father will not deny His children on earth the blessings that we seek and for which we hope. So long as we remain committed to asking for our needs and do not waver in our petitions to Him, we are assured of receiving answers to our requests. In the Sermon on the Mount, Christ challenges His believers to keep seeking God and to keep asking Him to continue working wonders in their lives.

SEARCHING FOR HEAVEN THROUGH THE NARROW WAY THAT LEADS TO GOD

> Matthew 7:13–28; 24:11; Luke 13:23–30; Acts 14:22; 20:29–31; John 15:18–20; Mark 8:34: 1 John 4:1; 2 Peter 2:1–3; Colossians 2:8; Mark 13:22–23

Christ does not want to keep those who gathered to hear His Sermon on the Mount in the dark as to the battle that lies ahead of them. He clarifies for them two different paths of life: the broad way and the narrow way. The broad way is the path of convenience that most people follow. It does not lead to heaven. The narrow way is the path that few people follow. It leads to eternal life, but only a few people are able to find it. He urges His followers to focus on the narrow way that leads to heaven and a certain meeting with their heavenly Father. Christ also admonishes His hearers to avoid following false prophets, those whose singular goal is to deceive. He encourages his followers to judge prophets not by their words but by the fruits of their actions.

Theme

JESUS, THE SOLUTION TO HUMAN TORMENTS

Text(s): Matthew 8:1–34

Lesson Introduction: Matthew chapter 8 reveals to us that Jesus has power over all things in this life. The power of His touch and/or His word can, at any point in time, accomplish whatever He desires to see take place. Not surprisingly, Jesus Christ has power over the sea, the wind, and all of nature as well. His authority over the universe qualifies Him to be our Lord and someone we can rely upon when we face adversity during the challenging times of life. It cannot be overemphasized that no other power in our world is able to achieve such great feats for humanity. Those who believe in Jesus Christ find in Him the power to overcome their struggles and their challenges.

BREAKDOWN OF THE STUDY

1. Christ's Power over Sickness and Disease
2. Christ's Power over Severe Natural Forces
3. Christ's Power over Stubborn Spirits

CHRIST'S POWER OVER SICKNESS AND DISEASE

Matthew 8:1–17; 9:1–6, 18–30; 15:30–31; Mark 7:32–37; Acts 3:6; 9:34

Jesus Christ manifests His divine authority through the power of His touch and His words. In Matthew 8:1–4, Christ touched the man who was a leper, and immediately he was healed of his leprosy. Likewise, in Matthew 8:5–13, Christ, while in Capernaum, met a centurion who approached Him with a request to heal his servant who suffered from palsy, a form of paralysis. Christ offered to go and see the servant, but the centurion insisted that Christ should "speak the word only," and his servant would be healed. Jesus Christ was amazed at the centurion's faith; He spoke the words, and the man's servant was healed "in the selfsame hour." In addition, Matthew 8:14–17 shares with us that Christ visited Peter's house where he found Peter's mother-in-law bedridden with a fever. When Christ touched her, the fever immediately left her.

CHRIST'S POWER OVER SEVERE NATURAL FORCES

> Matthew 8:23–27; Mark 4:39; Psalm 107:29; 29:10; 104:7–9; Nahum 1:4; Proverbs 8:29; Exodus 14:16

Because Christ's disciples had seen Him cure the sick and the lame, they were not shocked to see Him perform such miracles. However, His disciples did marvel at Christ's power over natural forces. For example, in Matthew 8:23–27, Christ was in a ship with His disciples, and He was fast asleep, but the disciples were facing a serious challenge because "there was a great tempest in the sea, insomuch that the ship was covered with the waves," and His disciples did not know what to do. Therefore, they came to wake Him up from His sleep, and Jesus manifested His power over natural forces by rebuking the wind and the sea; what followed was calmness. In other words, the wind and the sea recognized the authority of Christ and they obeyed His word.

CHRIST'S POWER OVER STUBBORN SPIRITS

> Matthew 8:28–34; 9:32–33; 12:22–24; Mark 1:27; 9:17–27; Acts 10:38; 16:18

A memorable event took place in the country of the Gergesenes (Matthew 8:28–30) where Christ and His disciples had an encounter with two people possessed with devils. And those afflicted ones were "coming out of the tombs," and they were "exceeding fierce, so that no man might pass by that way." Despite the fact that the devils were fierce and possessed uncommon power, they cried out for mercy when they spotted Jesus Christ. Those stubborn spirits were humbled by Christ's very presence, even though He did not touch them or threaten to punish them. In their fearfulness, they asked Christ to cast them into a nearby herd of swine. "And he said unto them, Go. And when they were come out, they went into the herd of swine: and, behold, the whole herd of swine ran violently down a steep place into the sea, and perished in the waters" (Matthew 8:28–32).

MAKING THE IMPOSSIBLE POSSIBLE BY FAITH IN CHRIST

Text(s): Matthew 9:1–38

Lesson Introduction: Faith is a requirement in the Bible to bring to pass the desire of a believer in Christ/God. Without faith it is difficult to please God and move Him to carry out our expectations of Him. However, when we are strong in faith and come to Him with requests, God is bound to deliver for us miracles that are impossible for anyone on earth to carry out. In Hebrews 11:6, the Bible states that "without faith it is impossible to please him: for he that cometh to God must believe that he is, and that he is a rewarder of them that diligently seek him." This quote means that one who seeks divine visitation from God must neither waver in faith nor doubt God's ability to do the impossible. Rather, the seeker of God must hold to Him in faith until divine involvement has taken place. Faith by the seeker is the act of doing what is believed to be impossible with men in order to achieve what is possible with God because of His superior nature.

BREAKDOWN OF THE STUDY

1. Faith in the Words of Christ's Believers
2. Faith in the Walk of Christ's Believers
3. Faith as a Windfall-Profit for Christ's Believers

FAITH IN THE WORDS OF CHRIST'S BELIEVERS

Matthew 9:18–21, 27; 8:1–2, 5–6, 24–25; 15:25; John 11:21–22; 4:47–49

The beneficiaries of God's power are those who know Him as Lord and Savior. Those people have relationships with Christ and worship Him alone as their Lord on a daily basis. Those who believe in Him know there is nothing impossible for Christ to achieve. Therefore, those believers have faith in their words when they reach out to Christ for help in their circumstances that need divine visitation. In Matthew 9:18–21, a certain ruler came to Christ after the death of his daughter to ask Christ to bring her back to life. The ruler said to Christ, "My daughter is even now dead: but come and lay thy hand upon her, and she shall live" (Matthew 9:18). These verses indicates that this ruler was a serious believer in the Lord and was aware of Christ's power having been demonstrated among those who trusted in His divine touch. His words were words of faith that moved Christ to act without delay to follow him.

FAITH IN THE WALK OF CHRIST'S BELIEVERS

Matthew 9:1–2, 18, 20, 27, 32; Mark 8:22; Acts 5:15; 2 Corinthians 5:7; Hebrews 11:27

Faith is an action that must be followed by personal engagement with Christ, the Deliverer. Those believers who encountered Christ walked up to Him and asked for help with their challenges. In other words, they sought Christ where He was and asked for His help. Verse 1 of Matthew chapter 9 tells us that some people who had faith in Christ brought a man with palsy (paralysis) to Christ with the strong conviction that Christ would heal him. Christ honored their faithful walk by healing the man of his paralysis. In verse 18 of Matthew chapter 9, the ruler walked to Christ in order for Him to bring his daughter back to life after she was declared dead. Also, the Bible records that the woman with the issue of blood for twelve years had faith to walk up to Christ and to touch the hem of His garment. James, the brother of Jesus Christ, states that "even so faith, if it hath not works, is dead, being alone" (James 2:17). This verse supports the fact that it is not enough to believe, but the seeker must take action.

FAITH AS A WINDFALL-PROFIT FOR CHRIST'S BELIEVERS

Matthew 9:6–7, 19, 22, 24–25, 29–30; 15:28; Mark 10:52

As recorded in the Bible, believers in Christ seemed to know the secret of receiving answers to their challenging needs. They knew the importance of confessing faith in their words and walking the walk of faith to achieve their desired result. Those people in Matthew 9 had windfall-profits for their words and walks of faith in Christ. For example, Christ healed the paralyzed man; the ruler who requested his daughter be brought back to life got the assistance he needed; the woman with the issue of blood for twelve years was happy for the miracle she received; and finally, the two blind men, who had both cried out to Christ for help, got the shock of their lives when their sight was restored. The encounters reported about in the Bible help us to understand that the approach to making the impossible possible in our own lives has not changed.

THE RESPONSIBILITIES OF THE TRUE CHURCH OF JESUS CHRIST

Text(s): Matthew 10:1–8

Lesson Introduction: The church of Jesus Christ is positioned to be a place of power, because Christ, as the head of the true church, is powerful. Also, Christ has given power to the true church to accomplish all her duties in the world. Power is what separates the real church of Christ from those churches that are powerful in their names but not powerful in what Jesus commanded His disciples to carry out among the people in the world. The Bible states that the kingdom of God is not in the words that we speak but in the demonstration of the power of God (1 Corinthians 4:20). For the true church to be relevant and impactful in this world, the power of service must be the foundation of the church. In short, souls must be empowered to respond to the gospel of Christ. The church is empowered to heal sickness and disease and to overcome unclean spirits that hinder people from serving God and living happy lives.

BREAKDOWN OF THE STUDY

1. Preaching about the Salvation of Souls
2. Possessing Power to Subdue Sickness and Disease
3. Possessing Power to Subvert Strange Spirits

PREACHING ABOUT THE SALVATION OF SOULS

> Matthew 10:1, 8; 28:19; Mark 6:7; 3:13–14; Acts 13:46–47; 2:41; Luke 24:47–48

The reason Jesus Christ called His twelve disciples to Himself was for them to assist in the work of evangelizing the people. The more hands there are in the work of evangelism, the better. In Matthew 9:35–38, Christ Himself spoke about evangelism and how important it was for more people to be involved in the work of soul winning. Christ enabled His disciples to be powerful and effective in ministering to the people they would encounter on their journeys. Christ understood that the disciples needed His power in their lives; otherwise, their efforts would be a waste of time and human resources. Likewise, to succeed in preaching to people today, believers in Christ must have time to pray and to fast so that Christ might immerse them in His power for preaching the gospel to people.

POSSESSING POWER TO SUBDUE SICKNESS AND DISEASE

> Matthew 10:1, 8; Acts 3:6, 16; 4:10; Luke 10:9; Acts 28:8; 19:11–12; 9:17–18; 1 Kings 17:20–22

The major assignment Jesus Christ gave to His disciples was to preach the kingdom of heaven to the people they encountered on their journeys. Jesus knew that His disciples would encounter people on their mission assignments who were battling sickness and disease. Such people were as deserving of the good news as anyone else, but they would have a harder time receiving it, if their focus was on their ailments. Therefore, Jesus gave His disciples the power to heal those who were sick and diseased. Christ knew that people who experienced His healing, through His disciples, would listen to the gospel message of the kingdom of heaven. We can deduce that possessing the power to heal the sick and the diseased will ease our ushering people into the kingdom of heaven.

POSSESSING POWER TO SUBVERT STRANGE SPIRITS

Matthew 10:1, 8; 2 Corinthians 10:4; Mark 3:13–15; Luke 10:19; Mark 16:17–18; Acts 16:18

Paul the apostle recognizes that the world we live in demands that true disciples of Jesus Christ possess the power to undo the works of the devil in people's lives. In 2 Corinthians 10:4, Paul declares that "the weapons of our warfare are not carnal, but mighty through God to the pulling down of strong holds." In other words, Paul tells us that the power Christ gives us is sufficient to pull down the power of Satan in any form or shape. Satan and his cohorts have kept many people in bondage against their will. And the only language that Satan recognizes is the language of a power that is higher and superior to his. Therefore, in Matthew 10:1 and 7, Christ tells His disciples that He has given them power to subvert unclean spirits. We have that same power, as we minister to people about the kingdom of heaven.

OVERCOMING CHALLENGES IN YOUR LIFE AND FAMILY

Text(s): Matthew 9:18, 23–26

Lesson Introduction: Human beings, who are created by God, have limitations as to what they are able to overcome or subdue when life presents challenges. However, if one has a relationship with the creator of the world, all of life's challenges can be overcome easily. A spiritual person understands his own natural limitations. The Bible states that "by strength shall no man prevail" (1 Samuel 2:9). This quote means that as human beings we are not able to deal with our challenges through our own strength. Our challenges are bigger than we are. But with the help of divine assistance, we are able to overcome challenges, irrespective of their magnitude or complexity. We know the Lord, who is able to overcome challenges at all times. Knowing Him and having a relationship with Him enable one to enjoy a consistently victorious and happy life.

BREAKDOWN OF THE STUDY

1. Possessing Uncommon Faith in Christ
2. Personal Understanding that Frees a Christian from Sorrow
3. Profound, Uncanny Faith that Connects with Christ for Supernatural Occurrence

POSSESSING UNCOMMON FAITH IN CHRIST

Matthew 9:18; Mark 5:22–43; Luke 8:41–56; Psalm 105:3–4; Galatians 5:6; John 6:68–69; 11:27; 1:29; 1 John 5:20

According to the Gospel of Luke, the ruler mentioned in Matthew 9:18 was Jairus, who was a magistrate. Jairus apparently knew that Jesus was a powerful individual who could heal all manner of sickness and disease—one who could even raise the dead. The unflinching faith that Jairus demonstrated in Jesus during a challenging time for his family is commendable. Such faith is recommended to anyone who seeks to have God's power demonstrated in their challenges in this life. The Bible tells us that without faith it is impossible to please God; for anyone who comes to Him must believe that He is a rewarder of those that diligently seek Him (Hebrews 11:6).

Seeking the Lord begins with repentance, followed by asking for forgiveness of sin and then placing your faith in Him. Only then do you begin to walk with Him on a daily basis and have a relationship in which Jesus Himself can testify that He knows you.

PERSONAL UNDERSTANDING THAT FREES A CHRISTIAN FROM SORROW

Matthew 9:18; 8:8–9; John 11:21–22; 9:31; Mark 9:23; Hebrews 11:17–19

Even as his family was challenged by the reality of his daughter's death, Jairus demonstrated a personal understanding of the power of Christ. His attitude following the death of his daughter was different from the attitudes demonstrated by his family, relatives, and neighbors. Even while they were mourning and lamenting the death of the young girl, Jairus sought out Jesus to worship him (Matthew 9:18). It may have appeared foolish for Jairus to seek out Jesus after his daughter was already dead, but, he did just that! The attitude that Jairus displayed indicates to all of us that he knew the power of Jesus. He refused to be filled with sorrow, because he knew someone who could bring his daughter back to life.

The lesson to be learned from Jairus is that possessing a personal understanding of Christ is important for us in order not to be cheated by Satan and his cohorts in this life. Our own personal understanding of who Jesus is will enable us to be calm and peaceful when others are fidgeting and worried about the challenges they are facing in their lives.

PROFOUND, UNCANNY FAITH THAT CONNECTS WITH CHRIST FOR SUPERNATURAL OCCURRENCE

Matthew 9:19, 22–25; John 11:22–23; Mark 9:23; Luke 5:19–24

Jesus knew that the young daughter of Jairus had died. Jesus also saw the enormous faith that Jairus placed in Him to be able to bring her back to life. Jesus did not question Jairus about his faith but immediately followed Jairus to his house. Christ does not question His believers who have great faith in Him. In another encounter with a faithful believer, the woman with the issue of blood for twelve years had faith in Christ, when she said, "If I could touch the hem of His garment, then I would be made whole" (Matthew 9:20–21). And again, a leper came to Jesus and asked Jesus to heal him of his leprosy. Christ, without hesitation, made haste to heal him because He saw the faith of the leper that he believed Him (Matthew 8:2–3). In summary, Christ sees our faith, and when He is convinced that we are truly focused on Him, He responds in ways that will surprise and amaze the people around us.

Theme

FULFILLING CHRIST'S MANDATE AND LIVING AS CONQUERORS IN THE EVIL WORLD

Text(s): Matthew 10:16–24

Lesson Introduction: Those who believe in His teachings and follow in His footsteps are Christ's disciples. Christ is the role model for all who profess Him as their Lord and Savior. In His earthly ministry, Christ was known to be a person of great strength; and yet, He was timid, humble, and gentle (Matthew 12:20). Christ did not project Himself to be someone of power and authority. Nonetheless, Christ was the wisest of all men who have ever lived. Even in our present dispensation there is no one who can match His wisdom. It was His wisdom that drew all categories of people to Him. In addition, Christ lived as a saint in the world. His entire thirty-three and one-half years on earth were free of sin, corruption, and guile, as noted by His disciples and those who encountered Him throughout His life. The qualities that Christ possessed are the same ones He expects His disciples to live out in this evil world.

BREAKDOWN OF THE STUDY

1. Sheep among Wolves
2. Serpents in Wisdom
3. Saints in the World

SHEEP AMONG WOLVES

Matthew 10:16; 26:65–66; Isaiah 53:7–8; John 19:7;
10:10; Psalm 22:12–21; 57:4; Revelation 1:9; Acts 20:29

Jesus Christ came into the world to fulfill what was written about Him. In Isaiah 53:7–8, the Bible tells us that "He was oppressed, and he was afflicted, yet he opened not his mouth; like a lamb that is led to the slaughter, and like a sheep that before its shearers is silent, so he opened not his mouth. By oppression and judgment he was taken away; and as for his generation, who considered that he was cut off out of the land of the living, stricken for the transgression of my people?"(KJV). In Matthew 10:16, Christ refers to the world as wolves and His disciples, who are reaching out to the world, as sheep. Christ knew that the world would be hostile to His disciples and would seek to destroy them. Nonetheless, the lifestyle that Christ lived among the people who were hostile to Him is the same lifestyle He calls His disciples to live in the world. Christ's disciples are His sheep in the world when they endure pain, persecution, and affliction in His name.

SERPENTS IN WISDOM

Matthew 10:16; 4:10–11; Genesis 3:1; 2 Corinthians
11:3; Revelation 12:9; Ephesians 6:10–17; 1 Peter 5:8; 1
Corinthians 9:25–27; Job 1:6–7; 2:2

Jesus Christ instructed His disciples to be as wise as serpents. Christ invokes the positive aspects of the serpent. Christ is telling His disciples to model the shrewdness of a serpent, by wisely avoiding the snares set for them as they take the gospel into hostile areas. Wisdom does not equal dishonesty, and innocence does not equal gullibility. Jesus showed that He was as wise as a serpent in the way that He taught. He knew enough to discern the differences in His audiences. For example, when the religious leaders caught a woman in adultery and brought this woman to Jesus hoping to hear Him condemn her, instead, Jesus declared that anyone who had not committed sin should be the first person to cast a stone at the woman. Upon hearing this wise response, the religious leaders who were present left one after another (John 8:4–8). Christ consistently demonstrated His wisdom by using this story-telling technique to teach and rebuke those with whom He came in contact. He refused to be caught in the many traps that His enemies laid for Him (Matthew 13:10–13; Mark 8:11; 10:2; 12:13).

SAINTS IN THE WORLD

Matthew 10:16; Philippians 2:15; 1 Thessalonians 2:10; 2 Corinthians 1:12; Hebrews 12:14; 1 Peter 1:15–16; Romans 12:18; Mark 9:50

In Matthew 10:16, Christ taught us how to optimize our opportunities to spread His gospel. Successful Christian living requires that we strike the optimal balance between the spirit of the dove and that of the serpent. God allowed the Spirit of God to come upon Christ in the physical appearance of a dove. In contrast with powerful birds of prey, doves have a meek, gentle, pure, and holy nature. They are beautiful, swift-flying birds that are entirely nonthreatening. Comparing the Spirit of God to a dove informs us that Christ wants His disciples to possess those attributes observed in doves as they relate to others.

CHRIST'S DEFENSES OF HIS IDENTITY IN THE WORLD

Text(s): Matthew 12:1–16, 39–42

Lesson Introduction: We live in a world where people do what they believe to be right before God; but unknowingly or ignorantly, they follow the path of perdition, because their ways are contrary to the teachings of Christ. Jesus's word to those who seek the truth is to search the Scriptures, because in searching they will find eternal life. The Scriptures testify to Christ being the One to believe and follow (John 5:39). Disobeying Christ, while carrying out rituals that are commanded by men, is a grievous offense and leads to eternal damnation. Those who find the truth enjoy liberty, peace, and joy, because they are free from religious confusion in this world (John 8:32).

BREAKDOWN OF THE STUDY

1. Christ the Personification of Perfect Worship
2. Christ the Preferred Prophet to all Other Prophets in the World
3. Christ the Preferred Wisdom to the Wisdom of Solomon

CHRIST THE PERSONIFICATION OF PERFECT WORSHIP

> Matthew 12:1–16; Revelation 19:10; Colossians 1:18; John 3:36; 5:21–25; 1:15; Galatians 3:24; 1 Corinthians 3:11; Acts 10:42–43; 4:12; Luke 24:47

Christ is the head of the church, and He is the embodiment of true worship. The head is the vital part of the body; it gives directions to all of the other parts of the body. Christ is greater than the temple and the Sabbath (Matthew 12:6). Therefore, Christ's ways are the model or yardstick of what pure religion entails. Believers need to heed His doctrines because He is the personification of perfect worship. Christ is a perfect representation of our heavenly Father on earth. In Romans 10:4, the Bible tells us that Christ is the end of the law. Conforming to and obeying all the religious rituals written in the Bible such as observing Sabbath days, holy days, baptism, and outward cleansing, without following the fundamentals that Christ commands, amount to a labor in futility. In Matthew 12:8, Christ declares that He is the Son of man who is the Lord even of the Sabbath day. Christ spoke these words in order to show the ignorance of the religious leaders concerning what it means to be the doers of God's word.

CHRIST THE PREFERRED PROPHET TO ALL OTHER PROPHETS IN THE WORLD

> Matthew 12:39–41; 28:18; Revelation 22:8–9; Mark 1:7; John 3:31; 8:23; 6:33; Romans 9:5; Philippians 2:9–11; Acts 10:43; Luke 24:44; 1 John 5:20

God approved Christ when He declared Christ to be His beloved Son in whom He was well pleased and when He commanded Christ's disciples to listen to Him (Matthew 17:5). In Matthew 12:39-41, the scribes and the Pharisees sought a sign from Christ to confirm that He was truly a prophet from God before they would believe Him. But Christ responded by referring to them as "an evil and adulterous generation" seeking after a sign. In other words, Christ was saying those religious leaders did not know God the Father nor did they recognize Him; and yet, they wanted a sign. Regardless of their request of Him, Christ emphasized that Jonah, the prophet, did not give a sign to the people of Nineveh; he preached a repentance message about the judgment of God that was about to come to pass in their land. And upon hearing Jonah's preaching, the people repented immediately, and God changed His mind about destroying their land. Christ declared that He was a greater prophet than Jonah, implying as well that His words must be believed without delay in order to avoid eternal judgment by God.

CHRIST THE PREFERRED WISDOM TO THE WISDOM OF SOLOMON

Matthew 12:42; 1 Kings 3:12; 10:24; 4:34; 1 Corinthians 1:30; Isaiah 9:6; 28:29; Colossians 2:3

According to the apostle Paul, Jesus Christ became God's wisdom, redemption, righteousness, and sanctification for those who believed in Christ's sacrifice on the cross (1 Corinthians 1:30). The wisdom of God described in this verse refers to the sacrifice Christ Himself voluntarily offered to God for the sin of the world. Christ described the wisdom of Solomon as meaningless and of no eternal significance when compared to the eternal redemption gospel message He was preaching to the people. Even though the wisdom of Solomon and his glory in this world brought the Queen of Sheba from the south to hear Solomon (Matthew 12:42), Christ informs the religious leaders that He is even wiser than Solomon and that they should pay attention to His gospel message.

RECOGNIZING DIFFERENT HEARTS IN CHRISTIAN MEETINGS

Text(s): Matthew 13:3–8, 18–23

Lesson Introduction: While teaching the people, Christ shared a parable in which He used the metaphor of a sower of seeds. The sower, who represents a preacher, sowed seeds, which represent the Word of God. Even though the seed that was sown was identical, the people who heard the Word of God processed it differently. The outcomes of the various sowings reveals the following: some people profited from the Word; some remained faithful to the Word for a short period of time; and others, while physically present, heard the Word but lacked the ability to comprehend it.

BREAKDOWN OF THE STUDY

1. The Swayed Heart
2. The Sensitive and Shallow Heart
3. The Succeeding Heart

THE SWAYED HEART

Matthew 13:3–4, 18–19; Acts 17:32; 24:25; 2:13; 2 Chronicles 36:16; 30:9–10

In the parable that Christ shared with the people, the sower was the preacher, who preached the undiluted Word of God to the people. In referring to the seed that "fell by the way side," Christ reveals that some hearts are not able to comprehend the Word. In Matthew 13:3–4, 19, Christ refers to the fowls (representing Satan) that devour the Word and sway the hearts of believers from understanding it. The "way side heart" is vulnerable and can be attacked by the enemy at any time, because it is weak. Christ is referring to those who are privileged to hear the Word of God in a tent meeting, church, campground, or religious gathering, but who are unable to receive its message into their hearts. Christ's observation of swayed hearts reveals a certain proportion of people we have in the church worldwide today. The swayed heart is the unserious person who is still does not know how important and crucial it is to know God and to be doers of the Word of God.

THE SENSITIVE AND SHALLOW HEART

> Matthew 13:5–7; 19:22; John 6:60–61, 66; 2 Timothy 4:10; 1:15; 2 Peter 2:15, 20–22; 1 John 2:19; 1 Timothy 6:10; Luke 16:13

In Matthew 13:5–7, Christ refers to two other hearts as "stony places" and "thorns." Those two hearts are similar because they are easily influenced by their environment.

First, Jesus deals with a group of people who He refers to as "stony places." They are stony places because the seed planted in them, the Word of God, lacks the soil to cover the seeds sown in this people. In other words, the spiritual soil, *prayer*, required to preserve the seeds is lacking. Consequently, the seed grows for a short time, but it then withers due to the scorching sun and shallowness of the soil. According to Matthew 13:20–21, people who have a stony heart receive the Word of God and are happy and joyful. But during tribulation and persecution, this group of people gives into pressure and backslides in their faith.

Second, Jesus speaks about the "thorns." The preacher sows the Word of God among the thorns. "Thorns," as used here, refers to people whose hearts are ambivalent to the Word of God. In Matthew 13:22, Christ declares that those thorns are hearers of the Word who, because of care for this world and the deceitfulness of riches, fail to live productive spiritual lives and consequently backslide. In summary, both the sensitive and shallow hearts believe in God but are not willing to pay the price (a prayerful life) to follow God and Christ in their walk with Him. It cannot be overemphasized that we live in a time where many who profess to be Christians are prayerless. In addition, these Christians spend so much time and effort in loving worldly things that they do not have adequate time to monitor their spiritual lives and their walk with God.

THE SUCCEEDING HEART

> Matthew 13:8, 23; Luke 8:15; Colossians 2:7; 2 Peter 3:17–18

Christ uses the term "good ground" to refer to those people who take in the Word of God and profit immensely from it. A person who is "good ground" has a heart that is receptive and exhibits all the good qualities that are lacking in swayed, insensitive, and shallow hearts. In Matthew 13:8, Christ shows that the same preacher sows the same seeds, but the hearers of the Word of God receive what they hear in good hearts (good ground). Christ's detailed explanation of a succeeding heart in Matthew 13:23 informs the hearers of the Word of God that the onus of getting the best from what they hear rests solely on them. The Word of God, when it is properly received, has the potential to multiply itself in the hearers thirty-, sixty-, or a hundred-fold. The succeeding heart as revealed by Christ reinforces Christ's words in Luke 13:24: "Strive to enter in at the strait gate: for many, I say unto you, will seek to enter in, and shall not be able." This verse shows that only those few Christians who are striving in prayer and continuing in the Word of God faithfully will succeed and live with God in heaven.

DETERMINATION TO LIVE A WATCHMAN'S LIFE FOR YOUR FAMILY AND THE CHURCH

Text(s): Matthew 13:24–30

Lesson Introduction: The understanding we have about Satan is that he is active and busy 24 hours a day. Satan does not rest as he is busy going "to and fro in the earth, and ... walking up and down in it" (Job 1:7; 1 Peter 5:8). Unlike Satan, after working a considerable number of hours, people are tired at the end of the day. Therefore, Satan appears to be winning or achieving his objectives over them because no one is able to match his spiritual work ethic. To prevail over Satan, one must possess a thorough understanding of Satan's scheme. One must then create a personal prayer strategy to counter Satan's constant, deceptive scheme. The prayer strategy must center on continually praying that Satan will not achieve his plans against one's family or the church of God. True Christians will not waver, will not tire, and will not falter; now will we be discouraged before Satan's plans are defeated.

BREAKDOWN OF THE STUDY

1. Personal Resolve
2. Primary Responsibility
3. Preemptive Responsibility

PERSONAL RESOLVE

Genesis 9:19–24; 1 Timothy 4:16; Job 31:1; Proverbs 23:31–33; Luke 9:62

Noah was the spiritual father of his home; and, he had a good working relationship with God. The prayer that Noah offered God after the flood, in the form of animal sacrifices, was accepted by God, and God said in his heart, "I will not again curse the ground any more for man's sake, for the imagination of man's heart is evil from his youth; neither will I again smite any more every thing living as I have done" (Genesis 8:21). Despite Noah's extraordinary relationship with God, Noah slacked off one time by getting drunk. Ham saw his father in his drunken stupor lying naked in his tent. Ham should have covered his father's nakedness; but, in a show of disrespect, rather than covering his father, Ham called to his brothers to see Noah in this compromised position. Without looking at their father's nakedness, Ham's brothers covered Noah. When Noah awoke, as punishment for Ham's offense, he placed a curse upon his youngest son, Canaan. In retrospect, if Noah had resolved to abstain from alcohol, the curse placed on Canaan and his descendants would never have occurred. One must resolve to be a disciplined spiritual person, if one is to prevail against Satan and overcome Satan's temptations in this life.

PRIMARY RESPONSIBILITY

Matthew 13:24; Acts 20:28; John 21:15–17; 1 Peter 5:2–3; Acts 13:2; Colossians 4:17; Proverbs 10:21; Psalm 78:70–72

In Matthew 13:24, Jesus shared the parable of the tares with His disciples and with the people who were present to listen to Him. The parable related the story of a man who sowed good seed in his field. The "good seed" is the Word of God, and the "field" is the faithful hearers who are under His care. We observe that this man was faithful and a diligent spiritual person, who did not fail to discharge his responsibility to his family or to the church the Lord had committed to his care.

Paul, the apostle, reminds the elders in the church to "take heed therefore unto yourselves, and to all the flock, over the which the Holy Ghost hath made you overseers, to feed the church of God, which he hath purchased with his own blood" (Acts 20:28). It cannot be overemphasized that being good spiritual watchmen is a responsibility that God has entrusted to His servants. In Christ's return to the world, after His resurrection, He spoke three times with Peter about the importance of feeding His sheep (John 21:15–17). True ministers of God must continue to feed the sheep under their care in order to help those sheep abide in the truth.

PREEMPTIVE RESPONSIBILITY

Matthew 13:25–30; Luke 22:31–32; 1 Peter 5:8; Zechariah 3:1; Job 1:6–12

Christ was a spiritual man and a responsible watchman. He was aware of Satan's strategy to cause people to disobey God's Word so that they would become alienated from God. In demonstrating His responsibility as a watchman, Jesus told Peter that He had prayed for him because Satan wanted to sift him as wheat (Luke 22:31–32). Christ's understanding of the enemy paid off, as Satan did not succeed in his quest to take Peter out of the kingdom of God.

Christ demonstrated before us that constant prayer is the key to derail the plans of the devil. In Matthew 13:25–30, Jesus revealed that, while men slept, an "enemy" came into the field to sow tares (weeds) among the good seed that had been planted. The servants of the householder observed that weeds were growing among the wheat and questioned their master. The master immediately recognized that an enemy had done this. But he told his servants that both the good seed and the tares should be allowed to grow until harvest time. In other words, the master recognized that he and his laborers had failed to be preemptive in watching over the field. By then, it was too late for preemptive action, because the enemy (Satan) had succeeded. The lesson for true watchmen is that they need to be responsible in taking preemptive action to protect their families and God's church against the intruder, Satan.

FACTORS THAT YIELD AN UNSTOPPABLE, FLOURISHING CHURCH IN THE WORLD

Text(s): Matthew 13:31–32

Lesson Introduction: The true church of God will not be hindered from reaching God's defined goals on earth. It is very sure according to Christ that the gates of hell will fight, but will not prevail against His church (Matthew 16:18). The gates of hell refer to Satan and his cohorts on earth. God's word about His true church can be relied on because God will stand behind His church at all times.

In Matthew 13:31–32, Christ reveals the essential truth about the church of God on earth. His word is comforting and encouraging to those whom God has called to raise the kingdom of heaven on earth for Him. In Luke 12:32, Christ states, "Fear not, little flock; for it is your Father's good pleasure to give you the kingdom." Christ is saying that His servants who are into sowing seeds (the Word of God) should not worry about the success of the work they do, because they are going to possess the kingdom of God (church) on earth. Also, His servants should not despise the days of small beginnings because the Lord rejoices to see the work begin (Zechariah 4:10). In other words, with the passage of time, the "little flock" will become a mighty flock, a congregation of the righteous to be reckoned with on earth.

BREAKDOWN OF THE STUDY

1. God Selects the Sowers for His Church on Earth
2. God's Sure Support of His Word for the Church on Earth
3. God's Metaphor of the Mustard Seed

GOD SELECTS THE SOWERS FOR HIS CHURCH ON EARTH

> Matthew 13:31; 28:19; John 15:16, 19; 13:18; 6:70; Acts 22:14; Jeremiah 1:5–7; Luke 6:13; Galatians 1:15

Jesus Christ gave the parable of a sower of seeds who was a skillful and knowledgeable farmer. In this metaphor, the sower represents those ministers of Christ who serve as His ambassadors, sharing their spiritual insight and understanding about building His church (the kingdom of God) on earth. Building the kingdom of God here on earth entails reaching the world just as Christ brought His disciples to follow and obey Him (John 1:41–45). The apostle Paul was called and approved by God to bring the Gentiles to the knowledge of the true God. Pairing with the other disciples, Paul was able to build the kingdom of heaven (church of God) on earth through evangelization. In summary, it is observed that the sower referred to in Christ's parable knew who was called to sow the good seed and when, where, and how to sow it. In the same vein, the approved messenger of God knows what to sow and what not to sow, along with when, where, and how to sow the seed for a rich harvest.

GOD'S SURE SUPPORT OF HIS WORD FOR THE CHURCH ON EARTH

> Matthew 13:31–32; 24:35; 5:18; Isaiah 42:21; John 10:35; Psalm 56:4; 2 Timothy 2:15

God has given His infallible Word (the whole Bible) to those He has called to be His representatives on earth. In Christ's presentation of the parable of the mustard seed, He described the mustard seed as the "least seed." This "seed" refers to the Word of God. The adjective "least," as used here, is significant. It is used in similar ways in other Bible verses. In Luke 9:48, Christ said, "For he that is *least* among you … shall be great" (emphasis added here and in the following verse). Also, in Matthew 5:19, Christ stated that "whosoever therefore shall break one of these *least* commandments, and shall teach men so, he shall be called the *least* in the kingdom of heaven: but whosoever shall do and teach them, the same shall be called great in the kingdom of heaven." Again, this verse shows the importance of *least* in God's vocabulary. God will stand by His *least* word (even the parts of the Word of God we may consider not to be important) and will hasten to fulfill it because He honors His Word more than His name (Psalm 138:2). Therefore, true ambassadors of Christ have a mandate to stick to the Word of God when reaching forth to the people on earth to build God's kingdom.

GOD'S METAPHOR OF THE MUSTARD SEED

Matthew 13:32; Daniel 4:12; 2:44-45; Ezekiel 31:6; Zechariah 8:20–23; Revelation 11:15

Christ's message about the mustard seed centers on the Word of God. In Matthew 13:32, Christ used a metaphor to describe the mustard seed, the herbs, the tree, and the birds. According to Christ, the tree is the church of God on earth, the birds are people who seek refuge in the tree, and the herbs are the people of the world who are non–Christians and enemies of the church of God on earth. Despite opposition from the enemies of God's church on earth, the church will flourish, and multitudes of people will find it to be a safe haven in all their circumstances and challenges in life. Praise the Lord; we have confirmation of the Word of God in God's church among us today. There are few churches that have God's approval and are discharging their responsibilities to those who need spiritual help in their challenges.

THE COSTS AND BENEFITS OF SEARCHING FOR GENUINE TREASURE

Text(s): Matthew 13:44

Lesson Introduction: Trace amounts of gold can be found throughout the earth and sea. However, large deposits of gold ore are seldom found near the surface; rather, locating significant amounts of gold involves a lot of hard work in the form of digging and drilling. In 1 Corinthians 9:24–26, the apostle Paul explains seeking genuine treasure in terms of cost and benefit. For those who are willing to bear the pain and expect the reward, Paul says, "Know ye not that they which run in a race run all, but one receiveth the prize? So run, that ye may obtain. And every man that striveth for the mastery is temperate in all things. Now they do it to obtain a corruptible crown; but we an incorruptible. I therefore so run, not as uncertainly; so fight I, not as one that beateth the air." Paul is describing the rigor that athletes subject themselves to in order to earn a corruptible medal. As hard as all athletes train, only one person gets the actual prize (gold). Nonetheless, Paul challenges Christians, like athletes, to take up the challenge, bear the pain, and run the spiritual race in order to obtain an incorruptible crown.

BREAKDOWN OF THE STUDY

1. The Price of Treasure
2. The Promise of Securing Treasure
3. The Profound Satisfaction of Securing Treasure

THE PRICE OF TREASURE

Matthew 13:44; Proverbs 2:1–5; Jeremiah 29:13; Deuteronomy 4:29–31; Luke 14:33; Acts 21:13

Christ's description of heaven shows the price to be paid to get there. Heaven is not a fairy tale or made-up story as some people would have us believe. It is a real place, and the price of admission to God's kingdom continues on earth until the journey of the pilgrim is over. In other words, the treasure of salvation must be kept and protected until the believer is no longer in this world. Christ compares the kingdom of heaven to a treasure which anyone who is interested must pursue wholeheartedly and without reservation (Matthew 13:44). The treasure of salvation is free, but an effort must be made to search for the true treasure on earth. In Jeremiah 29:13, the Lord says, "And ye shall seek me, and find me, when ye shall search for me with all your heart." In addition, in Matthew 7:7, Christ shows the importance of seeking. It is the hunger for and desperate quest to find the treasure of salvation that paves the way to this true treasure.

THE PROMISE OF SECURING TREASURE

Matthew 13:44; 7:7; Proverbs 8:17; 2:3–5; James 4:2–3; 1 John 3:22; Hebrews 11:6

Christ explained that the treasure was hidden but not to the extent that it could not be found. Even though it was hidden, the treasure would be found by the person who would not give up his or her quest to secure the hidden treasure (Matthew 13:44). Christ's words should make believers happy and encourage them to persist, since laying hands on the treasure is guaranteed. Securing the treasure results from constant prayer and making a determined effort to remain in the Lord.

In Matthew 7:7, Christ declares, "Ask, and it shall be given you; seek, and ye shall find; knock, and it shall be opened unto you." This statement confirms that His treasure is available to those who desperately want the treasure and are willing to persist in pursuing it. James 4:2–3 gives reasons why people who seek God's treasure may not receive it. According to him,

"Ye have not because ye ask not; and ye ask, and receive not, because ye ask amiss." Salvation seekers who do not receive the treasure either fail to ask for it, or they seek to use this treasure in the wrong way.

THE PROFOUND SATISFACTION OF SECURING TREASURE

> Matthew 13:44; 18:13; Philippians 3:7–9; Luke 15:32; 2 Timothy 4:7–8; Revelation 2:10; 1 Peter 5:4

Christ speaks about the joy that follows from locating the precious treasure. The precious treasure moves one to act impulsively, disposing of those material possessions that are far less valuable than the precious treasure of salvation (Matthew 13:44). The profound satisfaction Christ speaks about is the salvation of a soul, which results in both inward and outward changes. Living in compliance with Christ and opposing the world become paramount. The serious believer, happy with the newfound changes in his life, begins to see himself living out what the apostle Paul refers to in Philippians 3:7–9:

> But what things were gain to me, those I counted loss for Christ. Yea doubtless, and I count all things but loss for the excellency of the knowledge of Christ Jesus my Lord: for whom I have suffered the loss of all things, and do count them but dung, that I may win Christ, and be found in him, not having mine own righteousness, which is of the law, but that which is through the faith of Christ, the righteousness which is of God by faith.

CHRIST, THE ONLY TREASURE GENUINE CHRISTIANS NEED

Text(s): Matthew 13:44

Lesson Introduction: Genuine salvation is a treasure. Having a true spiritual treasure should lead one to abandon the mundane things of the world that compete with that precious treasure (Matthew 13:44). Most people who profess to have received the treasure of Christ's salvation seem not to understand the unmatchable value of that treasure. Some people have the treasure of salvation and still seek the treasures of the world. The spiritual treasure that Christ offers is sufficient unto itself. In Luke 14:26, Christ declares Himself to be that treasure when He says, "If any man come to me, and hate not his father, and mother, and wife, and children, and brethren, and sisters, yea, and his own life also, he cannot be my disciple." Christ must be the only treasure sought by those who testify to know Him and want to encounter Him in their lives. In Matthew 22:37, Christ is crystal clear when He says, "Thou shalt love the Lord thy God with all thy heart, and with all thy soul, and with all thy mind." This verse means that Christ expects true believers to accept Him as the ultimate treasure and to forsake all earthly treasures in seeking their eternal salvation.

BREAKDOWN OF THE STUDY

1. Believers with a True Treasure Jettison Adulterous Lifestyles
2. Believers with a True Treasure Jettison Covetousness
3. Believers with a True Treasure Jettison Pride

BELIEVERS WITH A TRUE TREASURE JETTISON ADULTEROUS LIFESTYLES

James 4:4; 1 John 2:16; Matthew 5:27; 2 Corinthians 6:14

The Bible condemns Christians who have adulterous lifestyles. God draws a parallel between Christians and the nonbelievers in this world. Those who are Christians possess God's treasure (Christ) in their lives. They are called to give full allegiance to the treasure He has revealed to them. To remain in true fellowship with God, Christ's believers must safeguard that treasure in their lives. Any relationship that compromises a Christian's allegiance to Christ must be avoided. In James 4:4, the Bible declares, "Ye adulterers and adulteresses, know ye not that the friendship of the world is enmity with God? Whosoever therefore will be a friend of the world is the enemy of God." This scripture verse tells those of us who have found God's treasure that we need to surround ourselves with others who have likewise received the treasure. Romantic relationships, business associations, and even close friendships with those who have not found the treasure of God in their lives can be dangerous. Those who place their earthly relationships over their relationship with God risk losing the relationship that they should most treasure.

BELIEVERS WITH A TRUE TREASURE JETTISON COVETOUSNESS

Matthew 13:44; 1 John 2:16; Galatians 2:20; Philippians 1:21

In Matthew 13:44, Christ illustrates, in the parable of the hidden treasure, what it means to have gotten the real treasure of God. According to Christ, a person who has found the real treasure would not covet other things in the world because nothing is greater than the real treasure he has gotten. The apostle Paul found the hidden treasure and said in Philippians 1:21, "For me to live is Christ, and to die is gain." Genuine believers, who have found the hidden treasure, take no interest in coveting worldly treasures that pale in value to the treasure God has given them. Again, the apostle

Paul vividly portrayed his attachment to this treasure in his life when he said, "I am crucified with Christ: nevertheless, I live; yet not I, but Christ liveth in me: and the life which I now live in the flesh I live by the faith of the Son of God, who loved, me and gave himself for me" (Galatians 2:20).

BELIEVERS WITH A TRUE TREASURE JETTISON PRIDE

Matthew 13:44; 1 Corinthians 4:7; 5:6; John 3:27; 1 Peter 4:10; James 1:17

The parable of the pearl informs us that God's spiritual treasure is like a pearl, precious and priceless. God's pearl is a treasure of inestimable value. No one can place a price on it. No one can purchase it. It is a gift from God. And because it is God's gift, those who have received this precious treasure should not act as though they have earned it. The apostle Paul asks those who feel pompous about God's precious treasure in their lives, "For who maketh thee to differ from another? And what hast thou that thou didst not receive? Now if thou didst receive it, why dost thou glory, as if thou hadst not received it?" (1 Corinthians 4:7). Christ is the true treasure given to believers. True believers accept the treasure of Christ's presence in their lives with humility and gratitude.

DUE PROCESSES IN THE WORLD BEFORE GOD'S FINAL SEPARATION OF SAINTS AND SINNERS

Text(s): Matthew 13:47–50

Lesson Introduction: Those who are in the church, who have experienced the salvation of Christ in their lives, have a mandatory responsibility to evangelize the world. Genuine converts are called upon to invite those who have not yet experienced conversion to join the church. In Matthew 13:44, Christ makes use of a simile when He likens the church to a net. In this parable, when the net was lowered into the sea it brought in all kinds of fish. In a similar way, the saved believers in Christ, who make up His church, serve as His net. We are responsible for drawing in all people through our evangelizing the world. Note that Christ uses the singular form of the word "net." This implies that that every saved believer in the church has an individual responsibility to bring people into the church. In this way, the entire church is responsible for the salvation of the world.

BREAKDOWN OF THE STUDY

1. Christ's Church and Its Special Calling
2. Converts and Counterfeits in the Church
3. Condemnation of Sinners and Crowns for Saints

CHRIST'S CHURCH AND ITS SPECIAL CALLING

Matthew 13:47; 28:19–20; Acts 2:38–39; 1:8; 13:46–47;
Luke 24:47–48; Isaiah 49:6

In Christ's parable, the fishermen use their net to catch every size and variety of fish. Once the net is pulled to shore, the fishermen separate the fish that are fit for consumption from all the others. The good fish are kept; the others are thrown back into the sea. Likewise, Christ sees His church performing the same role the net performs. The church pulls in men, women, and children of all races and nationalities. Christ's church is the only suitable organization in the world vested with that responsibility. Studying both the Old and the New Testaments reveals that God is most likely to commission those people who have a relationship with Him. In Matthew 28:19–20, Christ instructed His disciples to go into all nations to share His commandments and teachings with the people they came across. Christ has commissioned His church with that same responsibility.

CONVERTS AND COUNTERFEITS IN THE CHURCH

Matthew 13:30, 40-43, 47–48; 3:12; Acts 5:1–4; 1 Peter 4:17

The church building may be seen as a type of seashore. It is at the seashore that the fishermen separate the catch, keeping the good fish and releasing the bad. During Operation Go Fish, believers, in an effort to be soul winners, bring those they have met to the church building. Through the efforts of those believers, God will touch the hearts of some of the invited. In response they will believe the gospel, give their lives to Christ, and continue in the church as believers. Others who have been invited into the church are not yet convinced and will continue in their old ways, despite being in the church. In 1 Peter 4:17, Peter states that "the time is come that judgment must begin at the house of God: and if it first begin at us, what shall the end be of them that obey not the gospel of God?" The separation of the fish by the fisherman at the seashore shows that, when the net is cast, it will always draw in both the good and the bad together. Likewise, in the church, there are going to be true believers of Christ, along with nonbelievers and halfhearted followers of Christ.

CONDEMNATION OF SINNERS AND CROWNS FOR SAINTS

> Matthew 13:42, 49–50; 8:12; 24:50–51; Luke 13:27–28; 2 Peter 3:7; 2 Thessalonians 1:8; 2 Timothy 4:8; James 1:12; 1 Corinthians 9:25; 1 Peter 5:4

The parable of the fishing net is not meant to teach about fishing protocol. Rather, Christ uses this simile to show the responsibility of the soul winners to the lost in the world. The soul winners must draw into the church people of different backgrounds. As a result of Operation Go Fish, the soul winners will succeed in touching the hearts of some people who will genuinely surrender to Christ. However, that same net will draw in counterfeit believers who, for whatever reasons, will pretend to be believers. The parable of the fishing net assures us that a day of reckoning is coming when the saints and sinners will be separated, just as fishermen separate the good and the bad fish. In Matthew 13:49–50, Christ declares that the angels from heaven will participate in this assignment by severing the wicked from among the just in the church. In 1 Peter 4:17, Peter states that "the time is come that judgment must begin at the house of God: and if it first begin at us, what shall the end be of them that obey not the gospel of God?" The simple interpretation of 1 Peter 4:17 is that judgment will start in the church, which houses both the righteous and the unrighteous. The sinners will be condemned to hell, and the righteous saints will be privileged to live with God in heaven.

Theme

PHASES OF A TRUE SCRIBE

Text(s): Matthew 13:47–50

Lesson Introduction: The people God uses are not necessarily men or women of tremendous skills and abilities. Rather, those God uses only need to yield themselves to Him, and He will take over their lives so that they may serve humanity. The scribes in the Old Testament are people who were able to read and write. For example, Baruch was a scribe, a coworker and servant of Jeremiah in the Old Testament. When Jeremiah was put in prison, Baruch had to go to Jeremiah to transcribe Jeremiah's messages in order to share them with the people in the temple. In Matthew 23:34, Christ refers to some of His followers as scribes because of their unique understanding of the kingdom of heaven. Some believers are referred to as scribes, not because of their rigorous education or special skills but because they dedicate their lives to follow Christ. The title of scribe is earned by living a life dedicated to Christ. The title is forfeited the moment one strays from fulfilling that role.

BREAKDOWN OF THE STUDY

1. The Making of a Disciple
2. The Maturing of a Disciple
3. Mentoring a Disciple

THE MAKING OF A DISCIPLE

> Matthew 13:51–52; Luke 5:10–11, 27; 1 Kings 19:19–21;
> 2 Kings 3:11; Mark 16:15

Jesus Christ spent quality time with His disciples, teaching them about the kingdom of heaven. Christ also explained the mysteries of the kingdom of heaven to the people who were dedicated to Him. What set the disciples of Christ apart from others, who came to listen to Him, was their profession of faith in Christ as the Son of God. The disciples of Christ sealed their confession of faith in Christ by forsaking all, in order to genuinely follow the Lord (Matthew 4:19–20). In Matthew 13:51, when Christ asked His Disciples if they understood all that He had taught them, they affirmed their comprehension of the parables concerning the kingdom of heaven. The fact that Christ felt it necessary to teach His disciples helps us understand that people who have confessed Christ as the Son of God, and are His followers, must make themselves available to be schooled or properly taught. The importance of such teaching is to allow disciples to possess the knowledge needed to teach others.

THE MATURING OF A DISCIPLE

> Matthew 13:52; 2 Peter 1:18; Luke 8:51; Mark 9:2–31;
> Acts 9:4; 18:25

Christ's response to the disciples' answer in Matthew 13:51 reveals that He has seen His disciples as scribes (Matthew 13:52). Christ did not state this directly, but a true student of the Bible will understand Christ's mind that He is referring to His own disciples. To be a scribe means one possesses an uncommon understanding of the kingdom of heaven, understands the Law of God, and carries out that law. Recognizing that His disciples have attained this level of understanding, Christ refers to them as "scribes." Christ also refers to His disciples as "householders" (Matthew 13:52). The word *householders* implies that the disciples have the leadership abilities (authority, knowledge, and power,) to provide spiritual guidance to the people under their care. As leaders, the disciples had to continue to mature in their knowledge and understanding. Maturity is a combination of knowledge and experience. Knowledge is acquired through education and formal training. Experience is gained by being actively engaged in life and through encounters with a variety of people and situations. Knowledge and experience attained over a long period of time equip one for teaching others (Acts 4:13, 11:26). It is obvious that the disciples of Christ, having been His students and having accompanied Him throughout His public ministry, were qualified to teach His message to others.

MENTORING A DISCIPLE

> Matthew 13:52; Acts 18:24–26; 28:23; 8:31; 20:27; 1 Timothy 4:6; 2 Corinthians 3:6; John 21:15–17

Christ sees His disciples as resources who possess a wealth of information to lead other people. Mentoring of disciples has to do not with one's age but rather with possessing knowledge that others do not have. In Matthew 13:52, Christ relates how His disciples serve as scribes. His disciples possess a thorough understanding of the Scriptures and can lead people into the kingdom of heaven, either through engaging their listeners from the Old Testament teachings or by entirely teaching from the New Testament. The apostle Paul confirms the words of Christ when he states that anyone who is going to be an apostle, householder, leader, minister, or pastor must "study to shew thyself approved unto God, a workman that needeth not to be ashamed, rightly dividing the word of truth" (2 Timothy 2:15). Having a thorough knowledge of the Law of God and abiding by that law are fundamental to mentoring others who desire to be trained as disciples.

THE IMPACT OF CHRIST AND HIS FOLLOWERS IN THE WORLD

Text(s): Matthew 13:54–58

Lesson Introduction: Christ's intimate knowledge of the Word of God made Him a unique teacher, one who could demonstrate the Word of God perfectly, both in word and in deed. He had a profound impact on His generation. People who believed that He was of God were drawn to Him everywhere He went, except in His own country. While Christ astonished His countrymen with His teaching skills and His wisdom, He did not perform many great works among His own people. His countrymen had witnessed Christ growing up in their community, along with His family members (parents, brothers, and sisters). Their experience of His humanity blinded them to His divinity.

BREAKDOWN OF THE STUDY

1. Teaching the Word of God
2. The Temperament of God
3. Terrific Works of God

TEACHING THE WORD OF GOD

Matthew 13:54–55; 22:22, 33; Mark 6:2–3; John 7:15; Acts 26:24; 24:25

Christ possessed a complete understanding of the Bible. Moreover, He had the skills to deliver the Word of God with great impact. In Matthew 7:28–29, Matthew records that the people, including the religious leaders, were astonished by Christ's insights into the Word of God and His ability to explain it. Christ did not teach like the scribes, who received rigorous training under a religious leader. Rather, He taught with the authority of the Son of God. His comprehension of the Word of God caused the Jews to declare, "How is it that this man has learning when he has never studied?" (John 7:15 ESV). As Christians, we can amaze people with our understanding of the Scriptures. To do so, we must set our hearts to the purpose of learning everything that we can about God's Word as it is presented in the Bible.

THE TEMPERAMENT OF GOD

> Matthew 13:54–55; 17:27; Luke 4:22; 2:47; John 2:24; 16:30; 6:64; 1 Corinthians 9:19–22; 8:9; Romans 15:1–3; Titus 2:7–8

The word *temperate* refers to the disposition of one's mind. One's temperament can range from calm to extreme agitation and anger. Matthew 13:54 relates that Christ displayed a calm temperament while teaching in the synagogue. Even at the tender age at twelve, when Christ was first found teaching in the temple, He calmly listened to the doctors and asked them pointed questions. Jesus knew, from that early age, that He had to be about his Father's business of bringing the world to salvation. Christ's wisdom manifested in His attitude and comportment, both as a child in the temple and in His adult ministry. Christ was constantly aware of His mission on earth. The Bible informs us that Christ waxed strong in the spirit; He was filled with wisdom, and He had the grace of God upon His life (Luke 2:46-47). The combination of knowing the Lord personally, living in the spirit (praying and fasting), studying the Word of God, walking in the Word of God throughout one's life, and submitting to God will culminate in God's blessing His believers with wisdom.

TERRIFIC WORKS OF GOD

Matthew 13:54–55; Acts 9:32–35, 37–42; 28:8–9; Luke 8:24; John 2:2–6

"When he was come into his own country, he taught them in their synagogue, insomuch that they were astonished" (Matthew 13:54). The word *astonished* is the perfect word to describe Christ's impact upon the people He encountered in the temples and the synagogues. The people were astonished by Christ's grasp of the Word of God. They were amazed by His wisdom, as He taught them through sermons and answering their questions. They were stunned by His works as He healed the sick, raised the dead, and controlled the forces of nature. John 11:45 reports how, when Christ raised Lazarus from the dead, the people who knew that Lazarus's body had been decaying in the grave for four days were astonished when he came back to life and came forth still bound in his white burial wrappings. This miracle led many people to believe in Christ. The Bible tells of several other times when Christ brought the dead back to life. The Scriptures also recount for us that Christ's disciples, who learned from Him, astonished the people when they were able to raise those that were previously pronounced dead.

Theme

THE TRUTHS BELIEVED BY THE ADVERSARIES OF THE CHRISTIAN'S FAITH

Text(s): Matthew 14:1-2; Daniel 3:24-25

Lesson Introduction: The gospel of the kingdom of God will be heard in all the nations of the earth. The reason the Lord will allow the gospel to reach everywhere in the world is to quiet those who would say, on the judgment day, that they never heard the gospel (Matthew 24:14). The scriptures that are the basis of this study state clearly that Herod knew about the resurrection of the dead and about divine miracles. Likewise, Nebuchadnezzar witnessed the Son of God in the fire meant for Shadrach, Meshach, and Abednego. The cardinal teachings revealed in these interactions send strong messages: First, they affirm the fact that salvation is in Christ alone. He is the Son of God who became human to deliver those who were condemned to die by fire (Acts 4:12). Second, they testify to the fact that the dead will rise again—those who have done good unto the resurrection of life, and those who have done evil unto the resurrection of damnation (John 5:29). Lastly, they affirm the fact that healings or miracles are divine acts of God and not acts that human beings can carry out without God's involvement (Acts 3:12).

BREAKDOWN OF THE STUDY

1. Doctrine of the Resurrection of the Dead
2. Doctrine of Divine Miracles
3. Divinity of Christ

DOCTRINE OF THE RESURRECTION OF THE DEAD

> Matthew 14:1–2; 1 Thessalonians 4:13–18; John 11:11–44; Daniel 12:2

King Herod had John the Baptist beheaded. When Herod heard of Jesus Christ and the miracles He was working, he assumed that Jesus was John the Baptist "risen from the dead." In the language of the Bible, *raised*, *rise*, and *risen* are used in connection with resurrection (Matthew 27:52; 1 Corinthians 15:52; Acts 26:8). For example, in 1 Corinthians 15:12, the apostle Paul spoke to the Corinthian believers about Christ being raised from the dead, which to him meant *resurrection*. Christ was buried and on the third day, He rose from dead. Also, we learned that the disciples of John the Baptist came for the body of John to be buried (Matthew 14:12). There was no use of the word *revivification*. This clearly shows that Herod believed in the resurrection of the dead and that he believed in miracles. Jesus Christ demonstrated resurrection of the dead by bringing Lazarus back to life after his being in the grave for four days (John 11:11–44). Also, in this passage, Jesus said, "I am the resurrection, and the life: he that believeth in me, though he were dead, yet shall he live" (John 11:25). The apostle Paul, in 1 Thessalonians 4:13–18, assures believers that those who sleep in Jesus will rise up again as Christ the Lord will "descend from heaven with a shout, with the voice of the archangel, and with the trump of God: and the dead in Christ shall rise first." Paul's emphasis is on those who know the Lord and have relationship with Him.

DOCTRINE OF DIVINE MIRACLES

> Matthew 14:2; 2 Kings 5:10–14; Exodus 14:31; Acts 9:33–35; 8:13; Psalm 9:1

Divine miracles and healings are acts of God being carried out through human vessels. King Herod believed in the miracles that Jesus was reported to be performing, even though he attributed them to a resurrected John the Baptist. Divine miracles of God performed by His chosen ones are scattered through both the Old and the New Testaments. In the Old Testament, Elijah and Elisha demonstrated the power of God in their lives through the miracles they performed at different times. In Acts 10:38, the Bible tells us that God anointed Jesus of Nazareth with the Holy Spirit and power and that Christ went about doing good and healing those who were oppressed by the devil. This verse declares that God was with Christ, and that was the reason He was able to do what He did. In Matthew 10:1, Jesus Christ gave His disciples power against unclean spirits in order to cast those unclean spirits out and to heal all manner of disease and sickness. Again, this verse reveals that miracles are not what we can do on our own but that the power to do miracles is given by God to ordinary people. Therefore, it is wrong to conclude that the days of miracles are long gone. It is heresy not to believe in miracles, because that would contradict the Word of God.

DIVINITY OF CHRIST

Daniel 3:24–25; Luke 22:70; John 10:30; Romans 1:4; 1 John 5:9

Nebuchadnezzar claimed that he saw the Son of God in the fiery furnace meant for the destruction of Shadrach, Meshach, and Abednego (Daniel 3:24–25). The sudden addition of the fourth person in the furnace when three men were thrown in the fire was a divine act by God alone. God came to be with His servants who stood with Him in their faith against the order of Nebuchadnezzar to worship his god.

In the New Testament, there are references to confirm the divinity of Christ as the Son of God. For example, Nathanael referred to Christ as the Son of God, after Christ revealed Nathanael's identity as an Israelite indeed in whom there was no guile (John 1:47–49). John the Baptist recognized that Jesus was the Son of God when, as he was baptizing Him, the Holy Spirit came to rest upon Jesus (John 1:32–34). In Luke 4:41, the devils acknowledged Christ as the Son of God. Beyond the shadow of a doubt, the divinity of Christ as the Son of God confirmed by Nebuchadnezzar was not a false claim but a true revelation of God.

Theme

OVERCOMING CHALLENGES BY FAITH, PRAYER, AND PATIENCE

Text(s): Matthew 15:22–28

Lesson Introduction: The knowledge of this Gentile woman, who had an encounter with Christ, cannot be relegated to the background or swept under the rug. The Syro-Phoenician woman had to have known Christ well to have addressed Him as "Son of David." Also, she called Christ "Lord" three times in Matthew 15:22–26. Her knowledge of Christ's power enabled this woman to persevere in her request, even when rebuked by Christ and His disciples. True knowledge of Christ will always allow us to get what we want, regardless of how long it takes for an answer to come. Those who profess to know the Lord but give up on Him after a time do not sincerely know Him. The Bible states that "if thou faint in the day of adversity, thy strength is small" (Proverbs 24:10). This lesson is written to remind us that Christ said, "Ask and it will be given to you; seek and you will find; knock and the door will be opened to you: For every one that asketh receiveth; and he that seeketh findeth; and to him that knocketh it shall be opened|" (Matthew 7:7–8 NIV, KJV).

BREAKDOWN OF THE STUDY

1. Uncommon Perception of Christ
2. Unflinching Protest despite Criticism
3. Undeniable Performance by Christ

UNCOMMON PERCEPTION OF CHRIST

Matthew 15:22; 9:27; 17:15; 16:16; Luke 18:13; Acts 5:29; 4:19; John 11:27

Jesus left Herod's jurisdiction to retire to Phoenicia for a time of seclusion, because of the death of John the Baptist, who had been killed for his utterances against King Herod. Also, Christ had been rejected by the religious leadership of Israel during that period. Christ was seeking solitude. However, the Syro-Phoenician woman referred to in this text showed up to demand from Christ what she knew He could do for her. This woman perceived the power of Jesus and understood His abilities. The blessings we receive from the Lord are based upon what we believe Jesus Christ is capable of doing for us.

UNFLINCHING PROTEST DESPITE CRITICISM

Matthew 15:23–27; 9:27; Mark 10:47–48; Luke 18:35– 43; 2 Kings 2:1–9; Genesis 32:26

The stinging criticism the Syro-Phoenician woman faced from Christ and His disciples should have discouraged her. However, she was persistent in her request that Christ should deliver her daughter. It pays to stand up for your convictions and beliefs, despite people wanting to shut you down.

The attitude of the Syro-Phoenician woman must be emulated by Christians today. This Gentile woman continued to do the right things despite being rebuked. For example, she continued to worship Christ and seek His mercy.

In Luke 18:35–43, the Bible tells us about a blind man, who was always begging. When he heard a commotion, he asked what caused this sudden movement of people. He learned that Jesus Christ of Nazareth was passing by, and on hearing that, the blind man began to cry out, asking for Christ to help him with his sight. Despite criticism from the people around him, telling him to be quiet, this blind man ignored those voices he cried for attention until Jesus came to his aid. Again, there is no doubt about this blind man's knowledge about Christ. He would not be quieted, because he knew that Christ had the power to help him.

UNDENIABLE PERFORMANCE BY CHRIST

> Matthew 15:26, 28; 9:22; 8:13; John 4:50–53; Luke 18:42–43

According to verse 26 of Matthew 15, Christ refers to the Jewish people as His children and compares the Gentiles to dogs. Christ's seemingly harsh attitude was meant to test the faith of this woman, which was later rewarded by a miraculous healing. Christ's conversation with this woman can be likened to a delay in His answering our prayers. The woman continued to plead with Christ in an effort to persuade Him to heal her daughter. The answer to her prayer request came even as Christ was comparing her to a dog.

Today, there are people whose faith is not as strong as was this woman's. Believers need to be persistent, even in the face of being treated rudely or having to wait for God to answer their pleas. Like this woman, who did not surrender to despair, we must be constant in crying out to the Lord in faith. In Matthew 15:28, we are told: "Then Jesus answered and said unto her, O woman, great is thy faith; be it unto thee even as thou wilt. And her daughter was made whole from that very hour."

Theme

THE POWERLESS CHURCH AND THE POWERFUL CHURCH OF CHRIST

Text(s): Matthew 16:13–19

Lesson Introduction: The term *church*, as used in the Bible, does not refer to a temple, cathedral, or other magnificent worship site. Rather, the church is made up of believers who accept Christ as the Rock or Pillar of truth and as the Head of the church. The church of Jesus Christ is one where worshippers, regardless of the size of the congregation, confess Christ as the Son of the Living God. Such a church manifests the power of its founder, Jesus Christ.

BREAKDOWN OF THE STUDY

1. Confusion about Christ's Identity by Non-Disciples
2. Confession of Christ by the Disciples
3. Conferment of Power on the Disciples

CONFUSION ABOUT CHRIST'S IDENTITY BY NON-DISCIPLES

Matthew 16:13–14; 13:55; John 6:42; 9:22, 29; 7:12, 20, 25–27; Luke 22:67; 4:22

Christ's identity as the Savior of the world was not known by the people, the Sadducees, and the Pharisees who were the religious leaders of Jesus's day. While they had their synagogues and temples where they worshipped God; they were not disciples of Christ, and they did not believe that Christ was the "Son of the living God." Christ asked His disciples "Whom do men say that I the Son of man am?" And the disciples replied, "Some say that thou art John the Baptist: some Elias [Elijah]; and others, Jeremiah, or one of the prophets" (Matthew 16:13–14). The summary of Christ's conversations with His disciples about His identity, from our text, signifies that not knowing Christ as the Savior and as the Son of the living God robs those worshippers of the manifestation of God's power among them (Matthew 16:13–19). In our contemporary time, we have gatherings or assemblies that recognize Mary, the mother of Jesus, as the contact person between them and God. In Acts 4:12, the apostle Peter testified to the fact that there is no other name than Jesus Christ under heaven given among men whereby we must be saved.

CONFESSION OF CHRIST BY THE DISCIPLES

> Matthew 16:14–15; 14:33; 27:54; John 11:27; 1:49; Acts 9:20; 8:37; 1 John 4:15; Isaiah 26:4; 2 Samuel 22:3; Psalm 18:2

The disciples of Christ gave different names of what the people believed about Jesus: that He was John the Baptist, Jeremiah, Elias (Elijah); or one of the prophets. However, Christ wanted to know from His disciples what they thought of Him. Thus in Matthew 16:15, Christ asked His disciples the same question "But whom say ye that I am?" Immediately, "Simon Peter answered and said, Thou art the Christ, the Son of the living God" (Matthew 16:16). Because of Peter's confession, Christ now focused on Peter, since he had perfect understanding of Him (Matthew 16:16–19).

Peter's testimony of Christ helps us understand that there is no "general salvation." Salvation is a personal experience and not a group or multitudes experience. Everyone must be able to confess Christ as his or her Lord and Savior. For example, in Acts 2:38, "Then Peter said unto them, Repent and be baptized every one of you in the name of Jesus Christ for the remission of sins, and ye shall receive the gift of the Holy Ghost." This verse shows Peter addressing *everyone* in that congregation to make a *personal* decision to be saved by accepting Christ as the Lord and Savior.

CONFERMENT OF POWER ON THE DISCIPLES

Matthew 16:17–19; 18:18–19; John 20:23; Luke 10:19; 9:1; Mark 16:18; Acts 28:5; 8:5–8: 9:32–42

There is a difference between a powerless church and a powerful church. The Pharisees and Sadducees, who did not confess Christ as the Savior of the world and the Son of the living God, did not have the power that only Christ can give. Christ spoke to Peter and said, "I say also unto thee, That thou art Peter, and upon this rock I will build my church; and the gates of hell shall not prevail against it" (Matthew 16:18). A student of the Bible understands that "church" does not mean a building, but where two or three are gathered together in Christ's name (Matthew 18:18–20). Also, the "rock" that Christ spoke about was not Peter, as multitudes and Romans Catholics believe; rather, Christ is the rock, and Christ is saying that any person or group of people who confess Him as Lord is building on a rock.

Christ goes on to say, "And I will give unto thee the keys of the kingdom of heaven: and whatsoever thou shalt bind on earth shall be bound in heaven: and whatsoever thou shalt loose on earth shall be loosed in heaven" (Matthew 16:19). In Matthew 18:18, Christ conferred the same powers upon the disciples. By interpretation and application, believers who have confessed Christ and see Him as the Son of the living God are empowered to bind and loose on earth with God's backing.

Theme

QUALITIES RECOGNIZED BY HEAVEN THROUGH CHRIST'S TEACHINGS

Text(s): Matthew 18:1–6, 10; 16:16–19

Lesson Introduction: Heaven was important to Christ when He was on earth. Because He loved His disciples and those who came to listen to Him, Christ did not relent in emphasizing those qualities required of those who would be partakers of heaven. Christ promises His disciples and followers three things. First, Christ assures those who believe in Him that they will have the privilege of entering the kingdom of heaven. Second, confession of Christ will make His disciples and followers possess the keys to the kingdom of heaven on earth. Finally, Christ wants to see His followers exhibit the qualities that denote humility; meekness, selflessness, compassion, kindness, and nobility. It is the humble who will be considered the greatest in the kingdom of heaven.

BREAKDOWN OF THE STUDY

1. Personal Conversion in Christ
2. Public Confession of Christ
3. Proofs of Childlike Character

PERSONAL CONVERSION IN CHRIST

Matthew 18:2–3; John 3:3–5; 14:6; 2 Corinthians 5:17; 1
John 5:1; 2:21; Acts 4:12; 10:42–43; Mark 16:15–16

Christ's teaching on conversion centers on being born again. This conversion experience can happen at any point when a person is deemed to know right from wrong. Conversion and water baptism of infants or babies are not biblical, and they are not what Jesus demonstrated with His disciples. In Matthew 18:2–3, Christ called on a child that was available at the time to illustrate a point to His disciples. The child that was with the disciples had not reached the age of accountability and in the sight of God, such a lad is innocent, pure, and fit for the kingdom of heaven (Ezekiel 28:15; Matthew 19:14). Therefore, Christ wanted His disciples to have a born again or second birth experience. Nicodemus, a Pharisee, did not understand being born again as proposed to him by Christ. Nicodemus was confused when he said, "How can a man be born when he is old? can he enter the second time into his mother's womb, and be born?" (John 3:3–5). Rather, Christ requires that His disciples change their lives by seeing themselves as poor in the spirit and then mourn for their sins in order to be comforted and pardoned (Matthew 5:1–3). Living a new life begins at the point when we acknowledges our evil ways and make efforts to change our life in conformity with Christ's teachings.

PUBLIC CONFESSION OF CHRIST

Matthew 16:16–19; 14:33; John 11:27; 1:49; Acts 9:20;
14:15; Daniel 6:26

Christ does not encourage secret disciples. Christ wants to see that those who profess to know Him publicly identify with Him. In John 19:39, Nicodemus, a religious leader, a Pharisee, was a secret disciple of Christ. When he needed clarification about Christ, Nicodemus had to go to Christ in the night to meet with Him for fear of those in his religious sect seeing him with Christ (John 3:1–5). Nonetheless, the apostle Peter, among the disciples of Christ, openly declared Christ as the Lord and Savior

(Matthew 16:16-19). Peter's confession allowed Christ to declare that Peter would be privileged to have the keys to the kingdom of heaven on earth. Many times, Christ's disciples were apprehended for preaching the gospel of Christ and punished for their acts. Regardless, those disciples did not falter in the midst of persecution but counted it worth suffering shame for His name (Acts 5:40–41; 1 Peter 4:13–16; John 15:21). Confessing publicly that Christ is the Lord of your life gives God the glory for all your actions and may encourage others to follow Christ. Do not be a secret follower of Christ like Nicodemus.

PROOFS OF CHILDLIKE CHARACTER

Matthew 18:2–4; 23:11–12; James 4:10; Luke 14:11; 1 Peter 5:5

Christ used an actual child to teach His disciples a lesson about who is the greatest in the kingdom of heaven. The child that Christ used in His illustration was submissive, obedient, and willing to do everything Christ requested (Matthew 18:2–4). In other words, Christ's disciples and followers must possess a childlike character, which can be obtained by turning to the Lord to change their hearts (Ezekiel 36:26). The second work of grace that Christ wants to see manifested in a believer's life is referred to as *sanctification*. One who has been sanctified has a continuous thirst to be like Christ in separation from the world of sin and a relentless desire to grow in the Spirit (John 17:14, 16). In Galatians 5:22–23, the apostle Paul list the fruits of the Spirit to be desired in order to be seen as the greatest. The fruits of the Spirit are: love, joy, peace, longsuffering, gentleness, goodness, faith, meekness (humility), and temperance. The more a believer grows in *sanctification* (holiness), the more Christlike virtues that individual believer demonstrates.

QUALIFICATIONS TO STAND FOR CHRIST IN THE WORLD

Text(s): Matthew 18:1–6

Lesson Introduction: The commandment to go into the world and preach the kingdom of heaven is a mandate given by Christ to all His believers (Mark 16:15; Matthew 28:19). Prior to being sent out to reach the world for Christ, the disciples were instructed to take on those qualities Christ possessed when He was in the world with them. In Matthew 11:29, Christ declares to His disciples, "Take my yoke upon you, and learn of me; for I am meek and lowly in heart." Those who are willing to search and seek for those genuine traits of Christ will represent Him well. And the people they are reaching for Him will do well to hear and accept them, because they are truly from Him (Matthew 18:5).

BREAKDOWN OF THE STUDY

1. Salvation, a Prerequisite to Stand for Christ
2. Sanctification, Peculiar to Saints of Christ
3. Spirit-Filled, Proof of Servant of Christ

SALVATION, A PREREQUISITE TO STAND FOR CHRIST

Matthew 18:1–3; John 3:3; 2 Corinthians 5:17; 1 John 3:9; 2:29; 1 John 5:18; 1 Peter 1:3; Galatians 6:15

Christ was perfect in His teachings to His disciples, as well as those who came to listen to Him. When it came to teaching about the kingdom of heaven, neither did Christ contradict Himself, nor was he unclear. In Matthew 18:1–3, the disciples wanted to know who was the greatest person in the kingdom of heaven. However, Christ would not discuss greatness in heaven without making the subject of salvation (the passport to heaven) very clear to His disciples. In verse 3, Christ taught His disciples that "except ye be converted, and become as little children, ye shall not enter into the kingdom of heaven." Christ was unwavering about salvation as a requirement of entering the kingdom of heaven. Likewise, Christ's servants in the world today must have a genuine salvation experience in order to become Christ's ambassadors to the world. Sinners must repent of their sins in order to be used to reach the lost of this world.

SANCTIFICATION, PECULIAR TO SAINTS OF CHRIST

> Matthew 18:3–4; 23:11–12; John 17:16–18; 17:19; 1 Peter 5:5; Ephesians 5:26; 2 Thessalonians 2:23; 2 Corinthians 3:18

Christ's prayer to God for His disciples before departing the world was "Sanctify them through thy truth: thy word is truth" (John 17:17). To sanctify is to make holy, consecrate, dedicate, purify, and set apart. According to Christ, the only people who need a sanctification experience (the second work of grace) are those believers who have had a salvation experience. In other words, those disciples have encountered Christ in salvation through repentance and are saved from sin by the grace of God. In Matthew 18:2–3, first, Christ dealt with having a salvation experience (conversion) and then built on salvation by emphasizing the need to become as "little children."

Qualities that are common with "little children" include being humble, teachable, forgetful, forgiven, and tender of heart. Christ teaches that He wants His disciples to have the *humility* of children. What does it mean to be humble? Jesus is teaching His disciples to work on themselves by seeking those virtues devoid of ambition, pride, and haughtiness. In Philippians

2:7–8, the apostle Paul declares that Christ "made himself of no reputation, and took upon him the form of a servant, and was made in the likeness of men: And being found in fashion as a man, he humbled himself, and became obedient unto death, even the death of the cross."

SPIRIT-FILLED, PROOF OF SERVANT OF CHRIST

Acts 1:4–8; 2:17–19, 22; 15:12; 19:1–6; 11:15–17; 10:44;
Romans 15:19; Hebrews 2:4; 2 Corinthians 12:12; John 7:39

The promise of the Father, the baptism of the Holy Ghost, is the epitome of being called to represent Christ in the world (Acts 1:4–5). According to apostle Peter, Christ instructed the disciples to gather together in the upper room for God's divine visitation, at which they would receive power and possess the Holy Ghost. These manifestations of the Spirit are central to reaching the world for Christ. According to Acts 2:17–19, believers endued with power and the Holy Ghost from heaven allow God to "show wonders in heaven above, and signs in the earth beneath." In Romans 15:19, the apostle Paul revealed to the Romans what the Lord had done through him in propagating the gospel of Christ in different places. With the power of God and the Spirit baptism on his life, Paul had been able to impact the lives of people from Jerusalem all the way to Illyricum.

CHRIST'S UNCHANGING TEACHING ON MARRIAGE IN A CHANGING WORLD

Text(s): Matthew 19:3–11

Lesson Introduction: Christ was not appealing to the secular world in His teachings found in Matthew 5–19. Rather, Christ was teaching His disciples and others who embraced Him and showed interest in the things of the Spirit about how to live their lives in the world (Matthew 19:11). Marriage has been misconstrued, and the secular world wants us to believe that there is no blueprint for marriage. Regardless of what the secular world wants us to believe about marriage, believers in Christ, who have been born again and are walking with God on a daily basis, know that Christ's teachings on marriage are only meant for genuine Christians.

BREAKDOWN OF THE STUDY

1. Creation of Man and Woman
2. Causes for Creating Man and Woman
3. Consequences of Contradicting Causes for Creating Man and Woman

CREATION OF MAN AND WOMAN

Matthew 19:3–5; Genesis 1:27; 2:23; 2:18–20; 34:3; Malachi 2:15; 1 Corinthians 6:16; 7:2, 4; Ephesians 5:22–33; Mark 10:5–9; 2 Samuel 1:26; Proverbs 5:18–19; 12:4; 30:18–19; Deuteronomy 24:5

Christ applied the "law of first mention" in the Bible to answer the Pharisees who came to tempt Him (Matthew 19:4). The law of first mention is the principle that allows one to go to that portion of the Scriptures where a doctrine is mentioned for the first time and to study that first occurrence in order to get the fundamental, inherent meaning of that doctrine. Christ said to the Pharisees that in the beginning God created a man and a woman. The man and the woman that God created lived together as husband and wife (Adam and Eve). He did not create men and women to be separated or divorced from each other after a time. Christ's central message to the Pharisees is that "Wherefore they are no more twain, but one flesh. What therefore God hath joined together, let not man put asunder" (Matthew 19:6). God joined a man and a woman together; not two men or two women. By applying the law of first mention, the Bible does not support same-sex "marriage." Marriage in the "eyes of God" must be between a man and a woman.

CAUSES FOR CREATING MAN AND WOMAN

Matthew 19:3–6; Genesis 2:20; 1:28; 1 Corinthians 7:1–9; Malachi 2:15

Christ answered the Pharisees' question about divorce by applying the Scriptures.

The first cause or reason for creating a man and a woman is for the man to "cleave" to his wife (Matthew 19:5). The dictionary meaning of the word "cleave" is to stick to something like glue. In Genesis 2:18, the Lord God said, "It is not good that the man should be alone: I will make him an help meet for him."

The second cause is for the woman to help or support the man (Genesis

2:20). The man is not able to do everything, as the Bible shows in Genesis 2:20. The man needs help with less demanding tasks that the woman is able to provide. The concept of a man and a woman living together as a couple was given before the fall of Adam and Eve and not as a result or consequence of sin. In other words, marriage is God's ordained institution for how we should live together.

The third cause is for sexual intimacy (1 Corinthians 7:1–9). According to the apostle Paul, a man and a woman should marry to avoid fornication and adultery. Finally, marriage is for the purpose of reproduction (Genesis 1:28). God's design for a married couple is to multiply themselves in the world. It is through copulation by a husband and wife that God's goal of multiplication is achieved in the world.

CONSEQUENCE OF CONTRADICTING CAUSES FOR CREATING MAN AND WOMAN

> Romans 1:21–30; 2:5; 2 Peter 3:7; Matthew 25:31–36; Psalm 98:9; Romans 2:16; 2:5; Timothy 4:1; 2 Corinthians 5:10; 1 Corinthians 4:5

The apostle Paul addresses the issue of the world rejecting God by ignoring or abandoning His revealed truths (Romans 1:21–30). The heathen world has denied the existence of the righteous God, embraced the teachings of evolution and science, and worshipped creatures more than the Creator. By the heathen's logic, God has allowed His creatures the *permissive will* to carry out their desires as they choose. Permissive will makes man, and not God, sovereign. God is reduced to the role of a spectator or cheerleader. God's role becomes that of a helpless Father who, having done all that He can do, must now sit back and simply hope for the best. The heathen sees God conceding His sovereign power to His creation. This ghastly view is not merely a defective view of theism; it is unvarnished atheism. However, God has promised a day of reckoning when He will judge the world in righteousness by a man whom God has appointed in the person of Christ (Acts 17:31).

Theme

INHERITING EVERLASTING LIFE

Text(s): Matthew 19:16–30

Lesson Introduction: The rich young man who had an encounter with Christ wanted eternal life. In other words, the young man wanted to live forever. But the young man did not know that eternal life is a culmination of believing in the Lord and living a life on earth that is obedient to God. Christ began His answer to the young man's question by saying, "If thou wilt enter into life" (Matthew 19:17). There is a process by which one enters into eternal/everlasting life: The process of entering into life begins with a salvation experience. Through the grace of salvation, a person accepts the Lord as his or her personal Savior. The grace of God then enables the person to find the strength to keep God's commandments. The process continues when the pilgrim continues to seek heaven through detachment from earthly pursuits. The process is complete when the believer holds the things of this life with loose hands in order to follow the Lord wholeheartedly (Matthew 19:21).

BREAKDOWN OF THE STUDY

1. Priority of the Pilgrims
2. Predisposition to Possessions
3. Preoccupation with Preaching the Gospel

PRIORITY OF THE PILGRIMS

> Matthew 19:16–20; Hebrews 12:14; 1 Peter 3:11; 2
> Corinthians 7:1; Romans 6:22; Revelation 22:11–15;
> Psalm 34:14; 2 Timothy 2:22

The journey to eternal life begins at the point when a seeker separates from the desires of the world so as to pursue heaven. The saved individual (by the grace of God) looks for a city which has foundations, whose builder and maker is God (Hebrews 11:10). In Matthew 19:16–20, the rich young man Christ encountered wanted eternal life and had followed the commandments so as to attain it. Christ assured him that fulfilling external obligations alone (outward morality) would not lead him to eternity. Christ had earlier indicated to Nicodemus that he must be born again (Romans 3:20; Galatians 2:16). Christ instructed the young man that merely keeping to the letter of the law would not bring anyone to salvation. While abiding by the commandments listed in verse 18 provided the young man with God's grace, those commands focused only on his outward duties. When the young man protested that he had always lived by the law, Jesus revealed that the young man's real problem was his inward nature. Jesus had previously summarized the law in this way: "Love the Lord thy God with all thy heart" and "love thy neighbor as thyself" (Matthew 22:37). This was the young man's fatal flaw. His self-centeredness and desire for wealth and a luxurious lifestyle had blinded him to his real weakness. The young man's self-righteousness convinced him that he loved the Lord, but he loved his worldly wealth and possessions more than eternal life.

PREDISPOSITION TO POSSESSION

> Matthew 19:21–29; 4:10; 16:26; Joshua 7:21; Colossians
> 3:2; Luke 8:14; Timothy 6:9–10, 17; 2 Timothy 4:10;
> James 4:4; 2 Peter 3:10; Proverbs 11:28

Christ's conversation with the rich young man clarifies the fact that inheriting everlasting life does not come cheap. Christ's emphasis is on possession, because Christ knows that "no man can serve two masters: for either he will hate the one, and love the other; or else he will hold to the one, and despise the other. Ye cannot serve God and mammon" (Matthew 6:24). In Matthew 19:21–22, the rich young man became sad when Christ told him to sell all his possessions and to use the proceeds to meet the needs of the poor. Christ wanted the rich young man to divest himself of any hindrances to his seeking heaven. He wanted the man to focus on his pilgrimage to heaven; if the man was all about accumulating possessions, he would ultimately miss his goal of inheriting eternal life. Christ's message to the believers in the Bible and those who have the hope of heaven in them is this: "Love not the world, neither the things that are in the world. If any man love the world, the love of the Father is not in him. For all that is in the world, the lust of the flesh, and the lust of the eyes, and the pride of life, is not of the Father, but is of the world" (1 John 2:15–16).

PREOCCUPATION WITH PREACHING THE GOSPEL

Matthew 19:21–29; 28:19–20; Acts 1:8; 13:46–47; Luke 24:47–48

Christ's message to the rich young man was for him to first free himself from the entanglements of the world and then to come and follow Him. Following the Lord meant the rich young man needed to become a devoted disciple of Christ, preoccupying himself with the sole objective of preaching the gospel of the kingdom of God. The primary obligation of Christians is to fulfill the Great Commission. In Matthew 28:19–20, Christ instructed His disciples to go and teach all nations all that He had commanded them. The only people who are qualified to preach the gospel of Christ are those who are saved (those who have entered into the kingdom of God) and live holy lives on a daily basis. As they immerse themselves in the things of the Lord, their affection and love for God will be self-evident.

Theme

THE BIBLICAL TEACHINGS ON SECURING THE KINGDOM OF HEAVEN

Text(s): Matthew 20:1–16

Lesson Introduction: The parable of the laborers in the vineyard is intended to represent the kingdom of heaven. The focus of the householder, at the time of compensation, centered on the *quality* and not the *quantity* of the work done by the laborers. All the laborers got compensated because they worked, but the householder, who was a just, righteous man, knew what he was expecting of all the men he hired.

In this lesson, Matthew 20:1–16, the householder reveals three things: 1) the role of *grace*, 2) the role of *works*, and 3) the householder's *sovereignty*. The owner of the vineyard is the householder (Christ); the vineyard is the church. Christ recruited believers/disciples to work in His vineyard at different times. This passage, by interpretation, shows that some people are called to serve God very early in their lives, some people are called to serve God in middle age, and some are called to serve God when they are old. The irony in this lesson is that all the laborers received the same remuneration at the end of their day's work, regardless of the number of hours worked. This parable applies the saying "So the last shall be first, and the first last: for many be called, but few chosen" (Matthew 20:16).

BREAKDOWN OF THE STUDY

1. Salvation by Grace
2. Salvation through Works
3. The Supreme God and His Sovereignty

SALVATION BY GRACE

Matthew 20:1–16; 25:31–46; Ephesians 2:8; Acts 4:12; John 14:6; 1 Timothy 2:5–6; Mark 16:15–16; Hebrews 2:3

The parable of the laborers in the vineyard centers on the kingdom of heaven. The question is: How do we get into the kingdom of heaven? First and foremost, entering the kingdom of heaven is by the *grace* of God. As a result of Christ completing his mission, by dying on the cross of Calvary, God grants anyone salvation and makes anyone to be seen as a righteous person in His sight. Hebrews 9:22 declares that "almost all things are by the law purged with blood; and without shedding of blood is no remission." In other words, there is no salvation for anyone without Christ shedding His blood on the cross.

The disciples of Christ asked Jesus, "Who then can be saved"? Jesus answered, "With men this is impossible; but with God all things are possible" (Matthew 19:23–26). In Matthew 20:1–16, those who were hired to work in the vineyard of Christ benefited from the *grace* of God because they received full compensation for the day, regardless of the hours each worked. The first person who was hired was the last person to receive his compensation. Salvation is not by works, but the *grace* of God. He expected to be paid more, because he had worked longer. However, his compensation was based upon the just wage to which he had agreed.

SALVATION THROUGH WORKS

> Matthew 20:1–16; John 21:15–17; 2 Chronicles 31:20–
> 21; 2 Peter 1:5–10; Luke 13:23–24; 1 Corinthians 15:58;
> Galatians 6:7–9; Romans 13:11–14

Most preachers and teachers of the Word of God are slow to put emphasis on works to earn *salvation*. However, in Matthew 20:1–16, all the laborers/disciples/believers worked to earn their compensation. In other words, there is a direct correlation between the works one performs in the vineyard of God and salvation through grace. The church is God's vineyard; it is of His planting, watering, and fencing. We are all called upon to be laborers in this vineyard.

In 2 Chronicles 31:20–21, the Bible said of Hezekiah, "And thus did Hezekiah throughout all Judah, and wrought that which was good and right and truth before the Lord his God. And in every work that he began in the service of the house of God, and in the law, and in the commandments, to seek his God, he did it with all his heart, and prospered." Hezekiah worked for God on top of having relationship with God. Genuine Christians are known by the grace of God in their lives and by laboring for the kingdom of God on earth.

In Genesis chapters 12–14, Abraham made two geographical moves, built an altar and called on God, divided land with Lot to end a quarrel, paid tithes, and refused goods from the king of Sodom, choosing instead to rely on God's providence. He did all these works as an old man. After all these actions of faith, then he was declared righteous in Genesis 15.

THE SUPREME GOD AND HIS SOVEREIGNTY

> Matthew 20:7–8, 15; 8:11–12; Luke 15:11–32; 23:40–43;
> 1 Corinthians 15:9–10; Romans 9:13

The giving of a whole day's wages to those that had not done but a tenth of a day's work is designed to show that God distributes His rewards by grace and sovereignty. Laborers were called in the evening to receive their day's wage. Evening time in the Bible signifies a time of break from serious work and a time of rest without engaging in rigorous activities (Judges 19:16; Matthew 14:15). Evening time is the reckoning time for faithful laborers to receive their reward when they die.

The analogy is simple: the householder (Christ) calls the laborers (disciples/servants) to serve in the vineyard, and death calls them out of the vineyard to receive their penny. Though there be degrees of glory in heaven, yet it will be to all a complete happiness. The thief on the cross with Christ rebuked the other thief for talking against Christ, but he said to Christ, "Lord, remember me [in] thy kingdom." And Christ said to him, "Today shalt thou be with me in paradise" (Luke 23:40–43). The thief became a partaker of heaven without works, but by Christ's grace and sovereignty.

Theme

PREPARATIONS FOR DIVINE VISITATION

Text(s): Matthew 20:29–34

Lesson Introduction: The book of Matthew gives a record of two blind men meeting with Jesus. In the synoptic Gospels of Mark and Luke, the apostles indicate that only one blind man had this encounter with Christ. There is no reason to argue about who is right or wrong among the apostles; rather, students of the Bible must focus on how the blind person or persons changed their lives and regained their sight.

The faith that those blind men had in Christ was tested at the time Jesus was passing by. The multitudes cautioned them to be quiet; however, they refused to comply, despite the pressure from the crowd. Most Christians will be tested and tried during difficult times in their lives. There will be people who ask you to be quiet and live with your challenges. But the onus is on all Christians to desperately seek God's help with their problems. Every challenge in your life can be overcome, if you believe it is possible. God will always work with your faith to make the impossible possible. For there is nothing impossible to anyone who believes (Mark 9:23).

BREAKDOWN OF THE STUDY

1. Stability in Conviction
2. Staying Connected to Christ
3. Shrug off the Condescending Culprits

STABILITY IN CONVICTION

Matthew 20:29–31; 15:22, 25, 27; 9:27–31; Luke 7:6–7; Daniel 3:16–18; Joshua 24:15; Acts 5:29–32; Job 13:15

The two blind men were positioned at the right spot (by the wayside) so as to hear the movements of Christ and the people as they were all leaving Jericho. They were blind, but they had their ears to hear. Therefore, they used what they had to get what they did not have. In this lesson, we observe that those blind men were stable in their conviction that Christ could restore their sight. The men were probably blind from birth, yet they had faith to be healed by Christ. It is amazing to see the power of agreement between the two blind men. Both operated at the same frequency to receive from Christ the healing they sought (Matthew 18:19). "Without faith it is impossible to please him: for he that cometh to God must believe that He is, and that He is a rewarder of them that diligently seek Him" (Hebrews 11:6). It cannot be overemphasized that to receive the Lord's divine touch one must be stable, rooted, grounded in conviction, and built up in Him (Colossians 2:7). You may endure tests that cause you to waver in your faith or to stop trusting the Lord, but as you continue to believe and persist in your quest, the answer or solution to your challenge will come.

STAYING CONNECTED TO CHRIST

Matthew 20:30–34; Romans 14:8; Philippians 1:20; 1 Thessalonians 5:10; Acts 21:13

Unbelievable testimonies abound for both new converts and longtime believers who remain connected to Christ. It is easy to conclude that the blind men knew about Christ before they finally met Him and that they were waiting for an opportunity to meet Him and declare their faith in Him. On the day when Christ passed through where they were, their faith resulted in their having their eyes opened. Even though the multitudes of people with Christ discouraged the blind men from seeking Christ, the men were persistent and put up "prayers of importunity" in their asking to be helped. In Matthew 20:30–31, the blind men *cried out.* To cry out means to show persistence in asking to be listened to. In other words, the blind men prayed a prayer that Christ could not pretend not to have heard. Those blind men raised their voices, and Christ responded by asking them what they wanted from Him. Divine intervention is not peculiar to Bible days alone but happens in our dispensation, too. It is important to note that the blind men did not go through any pastors, overseers, superintendents, bishops, or evangelists to connect with Christ. Rather, both blind men carried out what the book of Daniel said, " The people that do know their God shall be strong, and do exploits" (Daniel 11:32).

SHRUG OFF THE CONDESCENDING CULPRITS

Matthew 20:30–31; Acts 21:13; 4:15–20; 5:17–25; Daniel 3:16–18

The attitudes of the blind men toward the multitudes traveling with Christ are worth emulating today. The multitudes believed the blind men were beneath their social circle because they were forgotten, common, poor people. They urged the blind men to leave Christ alone. Or they may have believed that Jesus had better things to attend to than to listen to people like them. Regardless of the attitudes of those condescending culprits, the two men, even though they were blind, could see that Christ regards all His followers equally. Christ's power is still present with us today to miraculously deliver the oppressed and those afflicted by Satan. However, to experience God's divine power in organized meetings, crusades, and living churches today, believers must tune out the multitudes who are not enjoying the spiritual experiences afforded to true believers.

Theme

FOCUSING ON JESUS AND DESIRING WITH A PASSION TO BE LIKE HIM

Text(s): Matthew 21:1–21

Lesson Introduction: Matthew chapter 21 is very similar to Matthew chapter 20, which we just finished studying. The apostles (Matthew, Mark, and Luke) present different information about the number of people Jesus encountered. In Matthew 20, Matthew speaks about two blind men, while Mark and Luke just mention one blind man. In our present lesson, we are able to see different versions as well. Matthew talks about a *colt* and an *ass* in his writing about Christ's triumphant entry to Jerusalem. But Mark, John, and Luke only describe Christ giving instructions to His disciples about securing a *colt* for Him to ride on to Jerusalem (Mark 11:4–8; Luke 19:32–35; Matthew 21:7; John 12:14). There is no doubt about the importance of the disciples of Christ preserving accurate information for the readers of the New Testament; however, it is meaningless and insignificant to worry about these trivial matters, when Christ, who is the key player, has a lot to teach us about Himself in Matthew 21:1–21.

BREAKDOWN OF THE STUDY

1. Meekness in Personal Character
2. Maintaining Proper Conduct
3. Mighty in Power in Curing and Comforting

MEEKNESS IN PERSONAL CHARACTER

Matthew 21:1–11; 11:29; Luke 14:8; Philippians 2:1–9; John 13:15; 1 Peter 2:21–23; 2 Corinthians 10:1; Numbers 12:3

Christ's meekness is demonstrated by the fact that he is righteous, humble, teachable, and patient under suffering. The Bible testifies to His meekness and humility in Zechariah 9:9. Christ demonstrates His meekness in Matthew 21:1–5, when He asks His disciples to make available to Him an ass and colt and not a horse. Horses are used by important people and kings, but Christ only asked for animals used by common people. In Jeremiah 45:5, God warned Baruch, the servant of the Prophet Jeremiah, about ambition and pride when He said, "Seekest thou great things for thyself? Seek them not." This teaching on *meekness* as a virtue of a true disciple of Christ must be taught regularly in the church of the living God. Servants of God and followers of Christ must imitate Christ's lifestyle of meekness. The apostle Paul preached about Christ's meekness and enjoined believers to learn of Christ. In Philippians 2:1–9, Paul speaks about Christ's humility (Christ avoided vainglory and strife, choosing to prefer others to Himself) and how God has exalted Him and given Him a name above every name.

MAINTAINING PROPER CONDUCT

Matthew 21:12–13; 1 Timothy 1:3; 5:7; Titus 1:9–11; Revelation 2:20; 2 John 1:9–10; 1:7

Christ is our perfect example of character and of how we conduct ourselves in all circumstances. Christ is gentle and firm. Christ is humble, lowly, and meek, but He frowns when people dishonor the name of the Lord or profane and desecrate things that belong to God. Christ's sudden switch from tolerance to righteous anger should instruct true representatives of God in the church. A church is a house of God and not a market for buying and selling. Nor is it a political institution where people campaign for office. The church is not a place for competition among members to flaunt who wears the finest clothes or drives the best car. Rather, it is a spiritual place to meet the heavenly Father and a place of orderliness. Therefore, a true servant of God is called to put things in order. In Matthew 21:12–13, Christ put things in order in the temple. In Titus 1:5, Paul said to Titus that he left him in Crete in order to "set in order the things that are wanting." Church administration and leadership are not roles for a weak or spineless person. An effective church leader must be a person of God who is able to discipline disobedient members and workers; detect false doctrines; teach correct biblical doctrines; and maintain order and decency.

MIGHTY IN POWER IN CURING AND COMFORTING

Matthew 21:14–16, 19–22; Acts 20:9–12; 10:38; 5:12; Luke 9:42; Mark 6:54–56; Romans 15:18–19; Hebrews 2:4; John 14:12

The manifestation of the power of God is a wonderful experience that should be enjoyed regularly in all the churches of the living God. The blind and the lame must have conviction that when they get to the church, they are bound to receive their miracles. In Jeremiah 8:22, Jeremiah asked the question "Is there no balm in Gilead; is there no physician there? why then is not the health of the daughter of my people recovered?" In this verse, the balm is the power of God, and the physician is Christ. And when Christ is present in His church, great things happen through His appointed servants in healing the sick and delivering the oppressed. The outcome of the divine power of God in His church is expressed through the manifestation of joy and happiness within the fellowship.

Theme

BIBLICAL MYSTERIES AND OVERCOMING RELIGIOUS STUMBLING BLOCKS

Text(s): Matthew 21:18–22

Lesson Introduction: In this lesson, students of the Bible will discover that the Bible is a spiritual book and should not to be taken literally. The Holy Spirit helps sincere believers interpret the Bible, by taking them beyond their human comprehension to understand its spiritual meaning. In Acts 8:27–31, a man of Ethiopia, a eunuch, opened the book of Isaiah and read at 53:7. Unfortunately, he could not understand its meaning. Regardless, God sent to him Philip, a servant of God, to guide, teach, and explain the verse to him and then led him to a salvation experience in Christ. In the spiritual sense, the Bible cannot be comprehended by unregenerate minds including Bible commentators (writers of Bible commentaries) who have not yielded or submitted to the God of the Bible. God only reveals deep interpretations of His Word to sincere seekers.

BREAKDOWN OF THE STUDY

1. Christ's Mission on Earth
2. Challenges to Christ's Mission on Earth
3. Christ's Means of Maneuvering on Earth

CHRIST'S MISSION ON EARTH

Matthew 21:18; 1 Corinthians 2:10–16; 1 Timothy 1:15;
John 12:46; 6:51; Hebrews 2:14; Luke 2:10; 4:18–19;
Isaiah 61:1–2; Mark 10:45

Matthew 21:18 tells us that Jesus became hungry in the morning. This verse is casually and literally translated, even by biblical scholars and commentators, to mean that Jesus was literally hungry and He needed food to satiate His hunger. But, the Spirit of God, in those who have the mind of Christ, reveals the deeper truth in the Scriptures (1 Corinthians 2:10–16). In John 4:34, Jesus explains to the people, "My meat is to do the will of him that sent me, and to finish his work." In other words, *my meat* means "my food, my daily routine/assignment," is to do the will of Him that sent me—to reach out to the souls of all mankind. This is Christ's most important mission on earth. Therefore, Christ gets up very early in the morning to carry out the will of His heavenly Father.

John 4:6 tells us that Christ was "wearied with his journey." In other words, Christ was tired. Because Christ was tired of His journey, He sat by the well. And Christ continued in His conversations with the Samaritan woman. It was during His engagements with the Samaritan woman that His disciples came to Him and said, "Master, eat," and Christ replied, "I have meat to eat that ye know not of." And the disciples said among themselves, "Hath any man brought him ought to eat?" And Jesus said to them, "My meat (my food) is to do the will of him that sent me, and to finish his work. Say not ye, There are yet four months, and then cometh harvest? behold, I say unto you, Lift up your eyes, and look on the fields; for they are white already to harvest" (John 4:34–35).

CHALLENGES TO CHRIST'S MISSION ON EARTH

Matthew 21:19; 23:23–25; Genesis 3:7; Hosea 9:10; Luke
13:6–9; 2 Timothy 3:5; Isaiah 29:13; Colossians 2:18–22

The fig tree has a symbolic meaning in the Bible and most references point to the nation of Israel. Fig leaves symbolize man-made religion and false righteousness. The Bible reveals that Jesus saw a fig tree in His way, and when He got to where the fig tree was, He saw leaves but no fruit (Matthew 21:19). Jesus used the fig tree to fully illustrate Israel's desperate condition. While the fig tree that Jesus saw had leaves, symbolizing outward righteousness; it bore no fruit. The godly virtues or fruits of the Spirit were lacking. In other words, Jesus saw religious people who had the outward appearances of men and women of God but who inwardly lacked godly virtues. In Genesis 3:7, Adam and Eve sewed fig leaves together to cover themselves after they had sinned. Adam and Eve covered their sin with fig leaves, but God saw their inward unrighteousness. It is clear that Jesus had a serious challenge with the false profession of faith of the nation of Israel. Jesus is aware that there are similar fig trees (Christians covered by fig leaves) in all the churches of the world today. Christians need to recognize and rebuke them.

CHRIST'S MEANS OF MANEUVERING ON EARTH

> Matthew 21:19–22; Hebrews 5:7; Luke 6:12; Daniel 6:10;
> Revelation 12:11; 1 John 4:4; 5:5; 2 Corinthians 10:3–5;
> Colossians 4:2

The fig tree represents the nation of Israel, which had practiced false religion for many years. The barren fig trees are the religious people who do not desire to be saved and enter the kingdom of God. They constitute a hindrance to those who truly seek salvation. Barren fig trees can be seen in many of the today's mega churches. Christ's means of dealing with such fig trees is to warn them to repent so as to avoid eternal damnation (Luke 13:3–9). In Matthew 21:19, Christ uses the symbol of the barren fig tree to foretell the final judgment that will come upon those who worship falsely; however, in Matthew 21:20–22, Jesus shares with His disciples the secret to overcoming such false believers. Christ taught His disciples to have faith and be prayerful. Therefore, if we are to root out barren fig trees in our mission to reach the world with the gospel of Jesus Christ today, we must have unwavering faith in God and remain prayerful. Jesus has declared, "All things whatsoever ye shall ask in prayer, believing, ye shall receive" (Matthew 21:22).

DESCRIPTIONS OF CHRIST'S UNLIMITED AUTHORITY

Text(s): Matthew 21:12–27

Lesson Introduction: Christ was in and out of the temple for three days, and His activities and undertakings stunned the chief priests, the scribes, and the religious leaders. Christ condemned, rejected, and rebuked their gross religious perversion of the temple. Questions were raised about who Jesus was and why the multitudes of people praised him by calling out, "Hosanna to the Son of David," thus indicating that Christ was the Messiah and Savior (Matthew 21:15). The religious leaders questioned this man who had no formal education or training in Judaism. They wanted Christ to defend Himself. In Matthew 21:23, the chief priests and the elders of the people asked Christ as He was teaching in the temple, "By what authority doest thou these things? and who gave thee this authority?" The religious authorities wanted to know what school Jesus attended; who was His teacher; and, under whose authority He was chastising the religious community. In this lesson, the Bible points us to Christ's unlimited authority in the universe.

BREAKDOWN OF THE STUDY

1. Christ's Authority as a Creator
2. Christ's Authority as a Confidant of God on Earth
3. Christ as the One Authorized and Central to God's Eternal Redemption

CHRIST'S AUTHORITY AS A CREATOR

Matthew 21:23; John 1:1–14; Colossians 1:16; 1 Corinthians 8:6; Hebrews 1:2; 1 John 1:1–3; Revelation 19:13

John, the Beloved, presents Christ to us as the Creator of the world. The Creator is referred to as the "Word" in the Gospel according to Saint John. And John reveals that the "Word" lived with God in heaven, and in the beginning the "Word" created all things, and without Him was nothing created (John 1:1–3). And the Bible says "The Word was made flesh, and dwelt among us, (and we beheld his glory, the glory as of the only begotten of the Father,) full of grace and truth" (John 1:14). However, the attitudes of the chief priests, the religious leaders, and the scribes in Matthew 21:12–45, who met Christ in the temple, demonstrate their complete ignorance of Christ's authority as the Creator of all things from the beginning. The books of John (1:1–2) and Genesis (1:1) share common phrases like "In the beginning was the Word" and "In the beginning God created the heavens and the earth." John 1:1–2 refers to the "Word" as Christ, and the *God* in Genesis 1:1, 26 and Genesis 3:22, is a plural form in Hebrew meaning "us" and "our." This usage signifies the first biblical hint of a triune deity (*trinity*), known in the New Testament as Father, Son, and Holy Spirit. Therefore, Christ was there in the beginning and was also a co-Creator of the world with God the Father and God the Holy Spirit.

CHRIST'S AUTHORITY AS A CONFIDANT OF GOD ON EARTH

Matthew 21:23; 3:17; 17:5; 12:18; John 12:28–30; 2 Peter 1:17; John 5:37; Isaiah 42:1

Christ received His authority on the basis of being the most trusted Son of God on earth. God the Father validated His close relationship with Christ when He affirmed and confirmed Him in the presence of Christ's disciples. In Matthew 17:5, the Bible tells us, "While he yet spake, behold, a bright cloud overshadowed them: and behold a voice out of the cloud, which said, This is my beloved Son, in whom I am well pleased; hear ye him." The closeness between God and Christ is that of father and son. God refers to Christ as His Son, and Christ refers to God as His Father.

The way and manner Christ and God related between each other confirm that Christ was loyal to God on earth, and there was mutual trust on both sides. In John 17:1, we hear, "These words spake Jesus, and lifted up his eyes to heaven, and said, Father, the hour is come; glorify thy Son, that thy Son also may glorify thee." The chief priests, scribes, and religious leaders did not understand that Christ, being the Son of the living God, had the right to everything on earth. God the Father has power/authority over all things; therefore, Christ, His Son, shares in all things that belong to the Father (John 3:35).

CHRIST AS THE ONE AUTHORIZED AND CENTRAL TO GOD'S ETERNAL REDEMPTION

Matthew 21:23; 1:21; Acts 4:12; 10:42–43; John 14:6; 3:36; 1 John 5:11–12; 1 Timothy 2:5–6

Christ is the perfect, authorized, and acceptable sacrifice for the remission of sin. Without Christ shedding His blood, there is no forgiveness of sin. God's love for the world is manifested as He witnesses His beloved Son suffer in agony in order to fully obtain eternal redemption for repentant sinners. The apostle Peter did not mince words when he declared to the religious leaders, scribes, and Pharisees that "neither is there salvation in any other: for there is none other name under heaven given among men, whereby we must be saved" (Acts 4:12). Christ assured His disciples before He left the world and those who believe in Him today, "I am the way, the truth, and the life: no man cometh unto the Father, but by me" (John 14:6).

Theme

WHY GENTILE NATION'S HERALD CHRIST AND FULFILL HIS COMMISSION ON EARTH

Text(s): Matthew 21:33–43

Lesson Introduction: In this parable, Jesus refers to the Jewish priests of His day, the scribes, Sadducees, Pharisees, and other religious leaders, as *husbandmen* and *builders*. It is the husbandmen and religious leaders who were in charge of advancing the vineyard (the church) of God on earth and receiving its fruits in God's name. These Jews had the privilege of sharing the gospel of Christ according to the revealed Word of God, but they failed to carry out this responsibility. Rather than committing to the task given to them, they went about preaching a gospel that would benefit their own interests. This failure by the Jews to take care of the vineyard (the church of God), and to produce fruits in the form of raising godly people in Israel, prompted Christ to hand down a verdict. The verdict Christ handed down was that obedient Gentiles (priests and religious leaders) would give recognition to the Stone (Christ) that was rejected by the Jewish people, as well as raise up people who would show genuine fruits of repentance through their walk as Christ's followers. Today, Gentiles around the world believe in the gospel of Christ and seek genuine fruits of repentance from those who put their faith in Him.

BREAKDOWN OF THE STUDY

1. The Chosen Gentiles
2. Carrying Out God's Mission in the World
3. Christ at the Center of the Gospel Message in the World

THE CHOSEN GENTILES

Matthew 21:41, 43; Acts 9:30–35; 8:36–39; John 8:25–29, 39–42; Galatians 3:8

Christ commissioned Gentiles to preach His gospel when he told the husbandmen and builders that "the kingdom of God shall be taken from you, and given to a nation bringing the fruit thereof" (Matthew 21:43). First, this word of Christ was fulfilled on the day of Pentecost. Those Jews from the diaspora, and other devout men, who came to observe the Feast of Weeks in Jerusalem became partakers of the power of Pentecost in their lives. A lengthy and impressive list of nationalities of those present took the Pentecost power to their Gentile nations (Acts 2:1–12). Second, Peter and John brought the power of Pentecost to the Gentiles in Samaria. Those Samaritans who believed the gospel preached by Philip received the baptism of the Holy Ghost and immediately became like the disciples of Christ who were endued with power on the day of Pentecost (Acts 8:14–17). Lastly, Cornelius and his household, Gentile people, became beneficiaries of the power of Pentecost. God's purpose for giving out His power to the Gentiles is to reach all the nations of the earth. In Matthew 28:18–19, Christ "came and spake unto them, saying, All power is given unto me in heaven and in earth. Go ye therefore, and teach all nations, baptizing them in the name of the Father, and of the Son, and of the Holy Ghost."

CARRYING OUT GOD'S MISSION IN THE WORLD

Matthew 21:34, 41, 43; 28:18–20; Genesis 12:1–3; Isaiah 6:8; Luke 24:46–48; Acts 1:8; 1 Peter 2:9–10; John 20:21

The parable that Jesus gave was about the husbandmen not bringing the fruits expected of them for watching over God's vineyard (Matthew 21:33, 41, 43). The husbandmen and the builders (Pharisees, Sadducees, scribes, and religious leaders) should have been leading people to God by being good examples to the worshippers, not preaching a message or gospel that would benefit their own interests. Since God's will for the world through the Jewish people was thwarted by the husbandmen and the builders, Christ gave a verdict that other nations of the world would rise up to carry out this task.

God's mission in the world is to bring all people to Himself. God started this mission with Abraham when He instructed him to leave his kindred and go to the land that He would show him and that all the peoples of the earth would be blessed through him (Genesis 12:1–3). In Matthew 24:14, God's plan for the world is that everyone on the surface of the earth will hear the gospel of Christ, and then the end will come. In the twenty-first century, Gentile nations of the earth are increasingly heralding the gospel of Christ. The Gentiles are the vessels who are seen reverencing Jesus Christ and working on His agenda for the end time.

CHRIST AT THE CENTER OF THE GOSPEL MESSAGE IN THE WORLD

Matthew 21:42, 44; Isaiah 28:16; 1 Peter 2:4; Romans 9:33; Ephesians 2:20

Despite Christ's rejection by the Jewish people (husbandmen and builders), Christ quoted Psalm 118:22–23, which speaks of Him facing rejection and His ultimate triumph. In Matthew 21:42, Christ said, "The Stone which the builders rejected, the same is become the head of the corner: this is the Lord's doing, and it is marvelous in our eyes." Christ's words above are words of confidence and certainty, and without a shadow of a doubt, most nations of the world have come to embrace Christ and see Him as the only begotten Son of the Father, the only sacrifice for the sins of the whole world, and the only One, by whom the believers in Him have faith to live with God in heaven. The apostle Peter declared in the presence of the religious leaders in Acts 4:11–12, when he was filled with the Holy

Ghost, "This is the stone which was set at nought of you builders, which is become the head of the corner. Neither is there salvation in any other: for there is none other name under heaven given among men, whereby we must be saved."

Theme

CHOOSING CHRIST OR FOLLOWING YOUR OWN WAY IN THE WORLD

Text(s): Matthew 21:42, 44

Lesson Introduction: Matthew 21:42 states that Christ is "the stone which the builders rejected, the same is become the head of the corner." In current terminology we render "head of the corner" as "cornerstone." This particular stone is not an ordinary stone, but the first stone laid at a corner that connects or joins two walls together, forming the foundation for the entire building. In this particular text, Christ is the cornerstone that connects man with God. Christ is the Reconciler bringing the world back to its Creator. Matthew 21:44 goes on to say, "And whosoever shall fall on this stone shall be broken." Anyone who comes to Christ broken—that is, humbled in His presence—receives pardon and forgiveness. Verse 21:44 continues, "but on whomsoever it shall fall, it will grind him to powder." Thus, the haughty and the proud have only themselves to blame when Christ wields His power and condemns them for their wrongdoings.

BREAKDOWN OF THE STUDY

1. Christ the Cornerstone of the Church
2. Compliance of Convicts to the Cornerstone
3. The Cornerstone as the Chosen One to Condemn

CHRIST THE CORNERSTONE OF THE CHURCH

Matthew 21:42; Isaiah 28:14–17; Ephesians 2:19–22; 1
Peter 2:4–8; 1 Corinthians 3:19–11; Acts 4:11–12; Psalm
118:22

The religious leaders of Christ's days (Pharisees, scribes, and Sadducees) can be likened to husbandmen, farmers who worked the land for the owner, the householder. In modern times, they would be referred to as *sharecroppers*. The parable in Matthew 21:33–39 informs us that the religious leaders of Christ's day had begun to act as though they were the property owners. They focused on themselves and advanced their selfish goals rather than those of the true householder and cornerstone, who is God. When these leaders rejected Christ, the cornerstone, He turned to the Gentile nations as a people who would make Him the Cornerstone and sure Foundation of His church (Matthew 21:42–43).

The word *cornerstone* can have any of the following meanings: foundation, bedrock, centerpiece, core, heart, base, backbone, key, or basis. All of these meanings connote that the church of Jesus Christ will have Christ as the center focus of worship. In Isaiah 28:14–17, Isaiah appealed to the leaders of Judah and Ephraim in Jerusalem to come to Zion, to a foundation he called "a stone, a tried stone, a precious corner stone, a sure foundation." In other words, the prophet Isaiah urged the people of Jerusalem not to seek protection from the Assyrians, but to come to the sure cornerstone, who is immovable, unfailing, and steadfast at all times. Christ is that Cornerstone, immovable and unfailing.

COMPLIANCE BY CONVICTS
TO THE CORNERSTONE

Matthew 21:44; Luke 19:8; Numbers 5:7; Isaiah 6:5–7

In His own words, Christ, the Cornerstone, offers mercy to anyone who falls on this Stone. In Matthew 21:44, Christ states, "And whosoever shall fall on this stone shall be broken." Christ's statement here means personal willingness to come to Christ for pardon and forgiveness. In addition, willingness to come to Christ will afford anyone a changed life completely different from their past life. In this verse we can also see that Christ will not force anyone to come to Him, as every individual has a prerogative or exclusive privilege to say either no or yes to Him. In this verse, a sudden transformation from being a wicked person to a broken, meek and humbled personality happens instantaneously. In the Bible (Old and New Testaments), brokenness is guaranteed to a convict who is genuinely sorrowful for his or her sins. God in His love will not turn away a convict, rather, He will show compassion and shower blessings on that individual (Psalm 51:16–17; 34:18). However, according to Jonah 2:8, those who come not with a genuine heart to submit to God forsake their own mercy.

THE CORNERSTONE AS THE CHOSEN ONE TO CONDEMN

Matthew 21:44; Luke 20:18; Hebrews 2:2–3; Daniel 2:34–35; Isaiah 60:12; Psalm 2:12

Christ was straightforward in telling his listeners the consequence of not coming to the Cornerstone to seek mercy. In Matthew 21:44, Christ says, "And whosoever shall fall on this stone shall be broken: but on whomsoever it shall fall, it will grind him to powder." Students of the Bible need to observe that Christ started that verse by explaining the right thing to do and then informed the hearers that neglecting option one only makes them victims of option two. Christ, the chosen One, is the only One to condemn and will act appropriately, as He has been mandated to carry out that responsibility by God (2 Corinthians 5:10; John 5:22, 27, 30).

Theme

THE KING'S INVITATION AND COMPLIANCE TO DEMAND FOR MEETING THE BRIDEGROOM

Text(s): Matthew 22:1–14

Lesson Introduction: Christ's parable in Matthew 22:1–14 shows diligent efforts by the king (God the Father) to reach those that were considered important (those that were bidden, that's the religious leaders) as well as those who were less important in the society. In Matthew 22:14, Christ summarized the foregoing parable by uttering the words *"For many are called, but few are chosen"* (emphasis added). Verse 14 helps Bible students understand that reputable or affluent people most likely will despise the gospel of Christ when it is presented to them (Matthew 19:23–24). Despite two different attempts by the king to reach those considered worthy, none of them made it to the dinner. However, those who were considered to be "bad" or unworthy (the Gentiles) gave heed to the call of the king and made it to the dinner properly attired.

BREAKDOWN OF THE STUDY

1. The Gospel for Men of Reputation
2. The Gospel for the Masses
3. Godly Garments for Meeting the Bridegroom

THE GOSPEL FOR MEN OF REPUTATION

Matthew 22:1–8; 21:36; Acts 11:19–20; 13:46; John 6:50–57; Luke 19:8–10

The parable of Christ centers on what God had done to bring the Jews (the nation of Israel and the religious leaders) to the Lord through His servants. His relentless efforts were frustrated by continuous rejection of God's invitation to fellowship with His Son. Christ likened the parable to the kingdom of heaven because the king desired those rich and recognized people in the society to witness the marriage of his son. Likewise, the disciples of Christ must be willing to share the gospel of Christ with the highly placed people in the society.

The word of Christ in Matthew 19:23–24 says, "Then said Jesus unto his disciples, Verily I say unto you, That a rich man shall hardly enter into the kingdom of heaven. And again I say unto you, It is easier for a camel to go through the eye of a needle, than for a rich man to enter into the kingdom of God." In other words, Christ says that there is no harm in trying to bring rich and highly reputed people to the Lord, but it will be hard for them to accept the gospel (the good news) of Christ. Consequently, in Matthew 22:6–8, those wicked rich, affluent people and religious leaders faced the wrath of the king for their wickedness. In the same vein, God's judgment looms over the unwilling rich, those of reputation, and religious leaders, who will despise the gospel of Christ.

THE GOSPEL FOR THE MASSES

Matthew 22:8–10; Luke 14:21–24; Acts 13:47–48; 18:6; 15:7; 28:28; Romans 9:24

The king's unsuccessful attempts to get invitees to attend the marriage ceremony of his son led to the king's turning to the commoners. In Matthew 22:1–8, by interpretation, God's plan was for the Jewish people to receive Christ, but the falling-out God had with the nation of Israel shifted God's focus toward the Gentiles. According to the apostle Paul in Romans 11:11–12, "I say then, Have they stumbled that they should fall? God forbid: but rather through their fall salvation is come unto the Gentiles, for to provoke them to jealousy. Now if the fall of them be the riches of the world, and the diminishing of them the riches of the Gentiles ….." Therefore, from our text, Matthew 22:8-10, God reached out to "both bad and good: and the wedding was furnished with guests." By interpretation, the commoners are the Gentile nations, which willingly accepted and embraced the gospel (good news) of Christ. Again, this is an indication to the disciples of Christ that reaching out to all men (both the bad and good) will in most cases lead to saving souls for Christ.

GODLY GARMENTS FOR MEETING THE BRIDEGROOM

Matthew 22:11–14; Exodus 19:14, 17; Revelation 19:6–9; 3:4–5; 16:15; 3:18; Ephesians 3:6

Bible students must fear at how the king approached the guest who wore no wedding garment during his brief appearance at the wedding reception. A proper wedding garment was a cultural requirement for attending a wedding. Any other garment rendered a guest unfit to meet the bridegroom. In the spiritual sense, those who were present at the wedding are referred to as the "Bride" and the "Bridegroom" as the Christ. In order to meet the bridegroom, it is important for the bride of Christ to have a garment of righteousness on that was given upon receiving the Son's invitation. The lesson to learn from Matthew 22:11–14 is that the brides of Christ must have Christ's righteousness in them upon receiving Christ's invitation. No other garments will replace the garment of righteousness in order to have fellowship with Christ.

Theme

CHRIST'S PLEASING GOD AND APPROVAL OF WICKED MEN

Text(s): Matthew 22:15–16

Lesson Introduction: It is a paradox that the Pharisees, who had malice and hatred for Christ, could still speak positively about Him. The Pharisees sought to discredit Christ by asking questions that called for answers that in turn would incur the wrath of the Roman authorities. They attempted to flatter Christ as described in Matthew 22:16: "And they sent out unto him their disciples with the Herodians, saying, Master, we know that thou art true, and teachest the way of God in truth, neither carest thou for any man: for thou regardest not the person of men." Despite the Pharisees being correct in their observations and analysis of Him, Christ knew their mission was insincere and intended as hypocritical flattery. Their mission was to make Him a traitor before the people and an enemy of the Roman authorities.

BREAKDOWN OF THE STUDY

1. Christ the True Messenger of God
2. Commitment to Teaching the Message of God
3. Clarity about Transgression of Everyone before God

CHRIST THE TRUE MESSENGER OF GOD

Matthew 22:15–16; 21:38; Malachi 3:1; John 6:38; 7:29; 3:16–17; 1 John 5:20; 4:10, 14; Hebrews 1:1–3

The Pharisees were learned men who practiced *separation from the heathen.* They affirmed the immortality of the soul, the resurrection of the dead, and punishment in a future life. They were the worst persecutors of Jesus and the objects of His strongest criticism. In Matthew 22:15–16, the Pharisees carefully rehearsed questions to ask Christ in order to trap Him and put Him at loggerheads with the Roman authorities and the people to whom He preached. The Pharisees offered high praise to Christ by calling Him "Master," meaning "teacher." They also called Him "true," indicating Christ was a true representative of God in the world. The Pharisees' positive words about Christ being the true messenger of God must not go unnoticed. It was not a cheap declaration by the Pharisees but an assertion based on what they had seen and observed in Christ. Therefore, the enemies of Christ and His followers must clearly acknowledge the servants of Christ as His true messengers in the world. Being "true" means possessing a genuine salvation experience, which uniquely prepares Christ's disciples to commit to the truth of the gospel of Christ.

COMMITMENT TO TEACHING THE MESSAGE OF GOD

Matthew 22:16; 13:54; 2 Corinthians 2:17; Ezra 7:6; Nehemiah 8:13; John 7:15; Acts 26:24

According to the Pharisees, Christ was a "true" person. This means that Christ was qualified to step in and teach the ways of God perfectly. The Pharisees and the Herodians said of Christ, "Thou … *teachest the way of God in truth*" (Matthew 22:16, emphasis added). The commendation about Christ could only have come from the Pharisees. The Pharisees were known to have given themselves to studying and teaching the law of the Old Testament. While they claimed the authority to teach, because of their acquired education, the Pharisees acknowledged that Christ had deep insights into the truth. ("Deep calls to deep," says Psalm 42:7 [ESV].)

The Jews also observed and marveled that Christ could teach without having had a formal education. But "Jesus answered them, and said, My doctrine is not mine, but his that sent me. If any man will do his will, he shall know of the doctrine" (John 7:16–17). Christ's word for the Jews and for those who desire to teach the Word of God is to be "born again" and steadfastly follow the Lord. God is committed to revealing the truth of His Word to such people.

CLARITY ABOUT TRANSGRESSION OF EVERYONE BEFORE GOD

> Matthew 22:16; Luke 20:21; 1 Thessalonians 2:4–5; Galatians 2:6; Acts 10:34–35; Mark 12:14; Job 34:19; 2 Chronicles 19:7

The Pharisees had great influence with the masses and were considered the highest religious authority by the people. However, Christ did not see them as true defenders of the truth but a bunch of hypocrites who followed man-made traditions (Mark 7:8). In Matthew 22:16, the Pharisees in their evaluation of Christ asserted that "neither carest thou for any man: for thou regardest not the person of men." Christ, as a true messenger of God, did not put a difference between the Pharisees and others, whether learned or unlearned, rich or poor. Rather, Christ was unsparing as He focused on anyone's transgression, including the Pharisees. Christ had condemned the Pharisees at different times for breaking the laws of God and found them to be sinners, too. The apostle Paul in Romans 3:23 clarifies that "all have sinned and come short of the glory of God." It cannot be overemphasized that God is still looking for men and women today who are true messengers of God. Those men and women are ready scribes (possess thorough knowledge of the Word) who will share the Word of God with people without fear or favor.

CHRIST'S TEACHING ON FUNDAMENTALS OF THE BIBLE

Text(s): Matthew 22:15–40

Lesson Introduction: Christ was called a "Master" by the religious leaders of His time, because of His perfect understanding of Old Testament law. When the Pharisees and Sadducees came to tempt Him, both groups met a man who was more than their equal. Each group came with a question that represented where their beliefs differed from Christ's teachings. Christ's responses exposed the error of their beliefs with truths that neither group could challenge or refute. The fundamental truths that Christ clarified for those religious leaders are the fundamentals that true Christians must commit to in this world.

BREAKDOWN OF THE STUDY

1. Balanced Teaching on Recognized Responsibilities
2. Bible Teaching on Resurrection
3. Basic Tenets and Role of the Redeemed

BALANCED TEACHING ON RECOGNIZED RESPONSIBILITIES

Matthew 22:15–22; Romans 13:1; Titus 3:1; 1 Peter 2:13–17; Proverbs 8:15–16; Ephesians 5:21; John 19:11; Daniel 2:21

Christ was more knowledgeable than the Pharisees, who were mostly lawyers and expert expounders of the Old Testament law. Their level of education is equivalent to that of a doctor of theology today. The Pharisees were at a crossroads about paying tribute to Caesar. They were looking for an answer to their own dilemma, and at the same time, they wanted to use Christ's own words to create problems for Him with the Roman authorities. According to Matthew 22:15–22, when the Pharisees came to the "Master" for a judgment as to whether or not it was right to pay tribute to Caesar, Jesus knew the intent of their heart and gave an answer that could not be faulted: "Render therefore unto Caesar the things which are Caesar's and unto God the things that are God's" (Matthew 22:21).

Christ's response was a two-part answer: First, because Caesar represented the Roman government, which coined the currency of the time, he had the right to tax those whom he governed. Likewise, today we are taxed by federal, provincial or state, and local government units. Those taxes, according to Christ, must be paid. Second, Christ disclosed that people must also give to God the things that are God's. What are things that belong to God? First, believers in Christ must offer themselves to God as a living sacrifice (Romans 12:1; 2 Corinthians 8:5). Second, believers in Christ must bring their tithes to God (Malachi 3:10; 2 Corinthians 9:6–8).

BIBLE TEACHING ON RESURRECTION

> Matthew 22:23–33; Psalm 17:15; 16:9–10; John 5:21, 29; 6:39; 11:23–25; Acts 4:2; 23:6–8; 24:15; 1 Thessalonians 4:13–18; 1 Corinthians 15:13–23

Resurrection is one of the basic doctrines of the Scriptures. Both the Old and New Testaments deal with this cardinal teaching. Believers in God, during the Old and New Testament dispensations, were not ignorant about resurrection after death. In 1 Samuel 2:6, Hannah, the mother of Samuel, declares that "the Lord killeth, and maketh alive: he bringeth down to the grave, and bringeth up." The prophet Daniel also realized that there was hope of resurrection beyond the grave when he said, "And many of those who sleep in the dust of the earth shall awake, some to everlasting life, some to shame and everlasting contempt" (Daniel 12:2 ESV).

In our text, Matthew 22:23–33, the Sadducees, who rejected the doctrine of resurrection, came to Christ hoping to disprove the doctrine by using an example based upon Mosaic Law. Christ, recognizing their intentions, said to them, "Ye do err, not knowing the Scriptures, nor the power of God" (verse 29). In other words, Christ said, the Sadducees lacked a full understanding of the Old Testament; they did not realize that God has the power to do all things, including raising the dead.

BASIC TENETS AND ROLE OF THE REDEEMED

Matthew 22:34–40; Deuteronomy 6:5; Leviticus 19:18; Galatians 5:14; Romans 13:9–10; James 2:8

Christ had a complete understanding of the Old Testament and how to apply it. Therefore, Christ answered the Pharisee who came to Him by referencing the Word of God, from Deuteronomy 6:5 (ESV), which states, "You shall love the Lord your God with all your heart and with all your soul and with all your mind" The compelling word from Christ to the Pharisee is *love*. Christ emphasized loving God with one's whole being (soul, heart, and mind). He stressed the importance of living only for God in the world, or better still, offering oneself as a sacrifice unto the Lord for one's whole life (Romans 12:1). The second law is closely connected to the first: "Thou shalt love thy neighbor as thyself" (Matthew 22:39). Truly loving God requires each of us to love all human beings, regardless of race, color, gender, sexual orientation, national origin, or physical challenges. Therefore, for the redeemed of the Lord, there should be no schism, favoritism, or racism against anyone.

SEEING AND SERVING CHRIST IN THE SPIRIT AS THE LORD

Text(s): Matthew 22:41–46

Lesson Introduction: While the Pharisees were gathered together, Christ seized the opportunity to address an important subject with them (Matthew 22:41). If Christ had not spoken to them at that time, the opportunity might have been lost. If there is a lesson to learn from Christ, it is that we must use every opportunity available to find out whether people know who Christ is. Christ's insight into the Pharisees' cluelessness of His true identity was confirmed. The Pharisees, who were the defenders of Judaism, did not recognize Him as the Personification and Embodiment of their faith. Just like the Pharisees of Christ's day, there are many modern defenders of Christianity who, unfortunately, do not know Christ as the Lord.

BREAKDOWN OF THE STUDY

1. Concentrating on the Validity of Christ in the World
2. The Confounding View of Christ in the Secular World
3. The Correct View of Christ in the Converted World

CONCENTRATING ON THE VALIDITY
OF CHRIST IN THE WORLD

Matthew 22:41–45; John 1:6–7; 8:14, 18; 15:26; 4:29, 9:25; Acts 4:12; Philippians 2:9–11; 1 John 5:9

Christ's focus was on the Pharisees, who were considered the arbiters of knowledge in their day. In other words, the Pharisees were seen to be the most accurate interpreters of the law. They were learned people with distinguished academic qualifications, similar to a person who holds a doctor of laws or doctor of theology degree today. That is why it was important for Christ to concentrate on the Pharisees and to challenge their perceptions of Him.

In Matthew 22:41–45, Christ asked the Pharisees questions about His identity. He asked them, "What think ye of Christ? whose son is he? … How then doth David in spirit call him Lord …? If David then call him Lord, how is he his son?" When pondering these questions, the Pharisees had no answers. They appeared to be overwhelmed by Christ's logical arguments and quickly succumbed to the wisdom of Christ's truth. As modern believers in Christ, we, like Christ himself, must strive to make Christ the central focus in our presentations of the gospel. Christ must be seen as the Savior of the world and the Lord of our souls. We must avoid the incorrect perceptions of some religious leaders, who still see Christ only as either the Son of Mary or the Son of David.

THE CONFOUNDING VIEW OF CHRIST
IN THE SECULAR WORLD

Matthew 22:42–43; 16:13–14; 12:23–24; John 10:33, 36; 8:41; Mark 2:7; 14:64

The Pharisees of Christ's day were religious leaders who possessed enormous historical knowledge of Judaism. Their acquired knowledge about God was not rooted in a spiritual calling but was based only upon their rigorous academic studies of the Old Testament. Those Pharisees studied Judaism only to become doctors at law, so that they could govern the people. Based solely on their studies of Old Testament genealogy, they only recognized Christ as the *Son of David*. The views that the Pharisees held are the same views the secular people of the world today have about Christ.

In Matthew 22:43, Christ spoke about David recognizing Him in the *Spirit, as Lord*. Christ's focus is spiritual and transcends the historical knowledge of the Pharisees. The Pharisees did not possess a spiritual understanding and were ignorant of the way of the Lord. According to 1 Corinthians 2:14, "The natural man receiveth not the things of the Spirit of God: for they are foolishness unto him: neither can he know them, because they are spiritually discerned." In this verse, the apostle Paul notes that an unregenerate person ("natural man") will fail to comprehend the things of the Spirit of God, because they have not had the illumination by the Holy Spirit.

THE CORRECT VIEW OF CHRIST IN THE CONVERTED WORLD

> Matthew 16:13–17; 14:33; 27:54; Acts 9:20; John 1:49;
> 6:69; 11:27; 1 John 4:15; 1 John 5:5, 20; Romans 1:4

The disciples of Christ were confirmed as walking in the Spirit, mainly by the apostle Peter's response to Christ's question. The disciples had experienced a spiritual conversion and believed Christ's teachings pertaining to the kingdom of God. To confirm their conversion, Christ wanted to hear from them their views about Himself. In Matthew 16:15, Christ asked His disciples, "But whom say ye that I am?" Peter answered for them: "Thou art the Christ, the Son of the living God" (verse 16). "The Son of the living God" means Christ is the only begotten Son of God, and He does not have any brothers or sisters (John 1:18; 3:16). The apostle Peter's testimony of Him proved to Christ that they knew Him in the Spirit, unlike the Pharisees. "And Jesus answered and said unto him, Blessed art thou, Simon Barjona: for flesh and blood hath not revealed it unto thee, but my Father which is in heaven" (Matthew 16:17). According to Christ, only God is able to reveal Jesus as the Son of God, the Lord and the Savior of the world.

Theme

TEACHINGS IMPORTANT TO CHRIST

Text(s): Matthew 23:23

Lesson Introduction: Christ, in Matthew 23, addressed the multitudes and His disciples about their religious leaders' lack of character by pointing out the errors of the scribes and the Pharisees. Christ's disciples and the multitudes needed to understand that they must *observe* and *do* what the scribes and the Pharisees taught (Matthew 23:1–3). However, those religious leaders must not be followed in their *works*, as they were very quick to preach what was acceptable, but failed to practice what they preached. Finally, Christ in Matthew 23:23 touches upon important teachings, "the weightier matters of the law," that the religious leaders are relegating to the background—judgment, mercy, and faith—while they are expending their energies on the lesser matter of collecting tithes of mint, anise, and cumin, which have no eternal values. The message of this lesson is the need to focus on things that are important to Christ. Obeying God's law, judging impartially, being merciful, and persevering in faith are serious matters for Christians to embrace.

BREAKDOWN OF THE STUDY

1. Forgiveness from God
2. Faith in God
3. Facing God's Judgment

FORGIVENESS FROM GOD

> Matthew 23:23; 1 John 1:7–9; 2:12; Colossians 1:14; 1
> Peter 1:18–19; Hebrews 9:12–15, 22; Ephesians 1:7; Acts
> 2:38; Titus 2:14

In this passage, Christ's focus is on the religious leaders who emphasized the people's tithing of their agricultural produce (which benefited them), rather than preaching on God's forgiveness to His people (Matthew 23:23). While tithing is an appropriate way to praise God, it cannot get anyone into heaven. Therefore, Christ's focus is on the weightier matters of the law: mercy, judgment and faith. Some Bible commentators believe that Christ spoke about *mercy* to encourage compassion among one another on earth. And while being merciful to one another is very important, Christ spoke about mercy in terms of His offering His blood as a sacrifice for humanity. Without His mercy, there can be no forgiveness of sins. God grants forgiveness to anyone who acknowledges their sins and comes with a repentant heart to Him. This message of *forgiveness* is timeless, and it is a message that must be preached until the end of the world. Christ's charge against those religious leaders is also an indictment of modern-day preachers. Preaching forgiveness through Christ must be at the forefront in gospel churches today.

FAITH IN GOD

> Matthew 23:23; Hebrews 11:6, 8; Genesis 15:6; 1 Kings
> 18:41–45; Galatians 3:6–14; James 5:14–18; Romans
> 4:3–6, 9

According to Christ, helping people to have faith in God in all circumstances of life is much more important than how much they tithe (Matthew 23:23). Constantly preaching on the need to tithe may lead believers to think that they can buy God's favor. This misunderstanding can lead Christians to doubt God's faithfulness when answers to prayers are delayed.

When the road ahead seems uncertain for believers and when the answers believers desperately seek are elusive, they need *faith* to get through difficult times. Faith is what enables believers to trust in the Lord to improve their present state. Faith is indispensable in our walk with God on earth. It is by walking in faith that believers receive answer to prayers and enjoy the blessings of God on earth. In Hebrews 11:6, the Bible states, "But without faith it is impossible to please him: for he that cometh to God must believe that he is, and that he is a rewarder of them that diligently seek him."

FACING GOD'S JUDGMENT

> Matthew 23:23, 33; Hebrews 9:27; Acts 17:31; 2 Peter 3:7; Romans 2:16; Psalm 98:9; 96:13; Jude 1:14–15; 2 Timothy 4:1; 2 Corinthians 5:10

Christ also ranks *judgment* as being weightier than preaching to people about tithing. Every human being has a pending appointment with Christ to receive His judgment. The Scriptures say, "It is appointed unto men once to die, but after this the judgment" (Hebrews 9:27). Christ's righteous judgment of all humanity is inevitable. In Acts 17:31, the Bible declares "He hath appointed a day, in the which he will judge the world in righteousness by that man whom he hath ordained; whereof he hath given assurance unto all men, in that he hath raised him from the dead." God the Son, Jesus Christ, is that judge (John 5:22). Believers and unbelievers will be judged by the perfect One who cannot be deceived (Galatians 6:7) and cannot be swayed by any prejudices, excuses, or lies (Luke 14:16–24). Therefore, Christ's message to the ministers of the gospel is to endeavor to focus less on tithing and more on what will benefit their congregations after this life is over.

Theme

BELIEVERS ENDURING GRACE IN THE MIDST OF DISCIPLES OF FALSE CHRISTS AND PROPHETS IN THE WORLD

Text(s): Matthew 24:4–5, 11–13, 23–24, 42–46

Lesson Introduction: The Bible has not kept us in darkness but has revealed that believers in Christ are Christ's disciples themselves (Galatians 3:29; 2 Corinthians 10:7). Being called Christ's disciples simply means that believers are able to do what Christ did in the world. However, Christ warned His disciples and followers in Matthew 24:5, "For many shall come in my name, saying, I am Christ, and shall deceive many." Christ's warning is that these false christs and false prophets will attempt to deceive people through demonstrations of signs and wonders. Those false christs and false prophets have only one goal: to deceive and mislead the true followers of Christ. Christ knows, however, that, in the midst of false christs and false prophets, there are believers who will endure to the end and who will be saved (Matthew 24:13).

BREAKDOWN OF THE STUDY

1. Deception by False Christs and Prophets
2. Deceiving Followers of Christ
3. Determination to Focus on Christ

DECEPTION BY FALSE CHRISTS AND PROPHETS

Matthew 24:4–5, 11, 24; Jeremiah 14:14; 1 John 2:18;
Acts 8:9–10; 5:36–37; John 5:43

Christ's words have come to fulfilment in our dispensation more than at any other time in history. There are people who proclaim that they are the real Christ, who has returned to the world. Also, there are those who declare they come in the name of Christ as Christ's disciples. Christ warns of those false christs and prophets, because they are deceivers. In Matthew 24:24, Christ says, "For there shall arise false Christs, and false prophets, and shall shew great signs and wonders; insomuch that, if it were possible, they shall deceive the very elect." In this present dispensation, there are disciples of false christs and false prophets who perform signs and wonders in an attempt to deceive people, especially Christians. Christians who are taken in by these impostors only encourage them and others like them.

DECEIVING FOLLOWERS OF CHRIST

Matthew 24:4, 11–12; Jeremiah 29:8; 2 Thessalonians
2:3; 1 John 4:1; Colossians 2:8; Ephesians 5:6; 4:14; 2
Corinthians 11:13–15; 2 Peter 2:1–3

Even though Christ's disciples were His faithful followers, Christ cautioned them in Matthew 24:4, "Take heed that no man deceives you." Christ's advice was intended not only for His disciples but for other believers who would come after them. Gullible followers of Christ are apt to focus on signs and wonders as the one sure standard of determining the true Christ's disciples in the world. In Matthew 24:11–12, Christ said, "And many false prophets shall rise, and shall deceive many. And because iniquity shall abound, the love of many shall wax cold." The enormity of the influence of the disciples of false christs and false prophets on the faithful followers of Christ should not be underestimated. First, the faithful followers will chase after signs and wonders. Second, they will focus more on things of this world and care less for heaven. Third, their faith in Christ will dwindle greatly. Lastly, they will relapse into their former bad ways.

DETERMINATION TO FOCUS ON CHRIST

Matthew 24:13, 42–46; 1 Corinthians 9:24–27; Hebrews
12:1–2; 3:14; Revelation 2:10; Luke 8:15

Christ's words to His disciples and to other believers in Him are meant to alert them to the diabolical ways of false christs and false prophets. To be forewarned is to be forearmed. In Matthew 24:13, Christ said, "But he that shall endure unto the end, the same shall be saved." The salient word in this verse is *endure*. Endurance means persevering in faith always, studying the Word of God, and praying without ceasing. In Matthew 24:42–46, Christ exhorted His disciples to be diligent in watching carefully for false christs and prophets, whom He refers to as thieves, so that they may not rob them of salvation, which is their reward for enduring and persevering in the faith.

Theme

CHRIST'S COUNSELS ON MAKING HEAVEN WITH ETERNAL ENDURING REWARD

Text(s): Matthew 24:34–47

Lesson Introduction: Christ's words in Matthew 24:35 show He is switching gears and ready to focus on another topic of interest. In Matthew 24:1–34, Christ spent considerable time highlighting the signs of the last days. He concluded that topic by declaring, "Verily I say unto you, This generation shall not pass, till all these things be fulfilled" (Matthew 24:34). We must be convinced that Christ meant exactly what He said, that this generation shall not pass away until all that He has said is fulfilled (Matthew 24:35). In verses 35–47, Christ counsels His disciples and followers as to what they must do to be partakers of heaven. According to Christ, nobody, not even His disciples and followers, gets to heaven by sitting on their hands and waiting; each of us must make an effort to get there. Heaven is earned by following Christ closely and pleasing the Lord at all times, to the end.

BREAKDOWN OF THE STUDY

1. Prioritizing Following Christ over Corruptions in the World
2. Putting our Focus on Christian's Commitment and Consecration in the World
3. Present Forbearances that Fit with Christ's Compensation

PRIORITIZING FOLLOWING CHRIST OVER CORRUPTIONS IN THE WORLD

Matthew 24:35–43; 6:24; 1 John 2:15–17; Romans 12:2; 13:14; Colossians 3:1–2; Jude 1:16–18; 1 Peter 4:2–3; 2:11; Titus 2:12; Galatians 5:24

Christ's counsel to His disciples and followers is to distinguish themselves from those people of the world whose focus is solely on earthly things. According to Christ in Matthew 24:35–43, the Lord will come when least expected. For example, the people who lived during the time of Noah were busy engaging in the things of the world and not focused on their relationship with God. They were "eating and drinking, marrying and giving in marriage" (Matthew 24:38). Because of their worldly focus, the people were not aware of Noah's preparations and departure into the ark, until after he had left. The examples given by Christ show that being caught up in the routines of everyday life can dull people's consciousness to important events happening around them. Believers must be spiritually alert and be rapture-ready, in case the trumpet of the Lord sounds. Only those who hear the trumpet of the Lord will go to heaven with Him.

PUTTING OUR FOCUS ON CHRISTIAN'S COMMITMENT AND CONSECRATION IN THE WORLD

Matthew 24:44; 25:1–13; Romans 12:1; 1 Peter 4:2; 2:24; Colossians 1:10; Ephesians 4:15; Philippians 3:8; 2 Peter 3:18; Ruth 1:15–16; Joshua 24:15

Christ's counsel for His disciples and followers is to be *ready*. Readiness does not imply physical preparations (taking a bath and putting on clothes) but connotes spiritual preparations. In Matthew 25:1–13, Christ shared the parable of ten virgins who were waiting for the bridegroom. According to Christ, five of the virgins were wise and the other five were foolish. This particular parable has to do with ten people who were waiting for the Lord to come and receive them to Himself (the Bridegroom). Unfortunately, the five foolish virgins did not have sufficient *oil* to keep the *lamp* burning until the Bridegroom arrived.

In this story, believers are the lamps, and the oil is both the salvation experience and other spiritual endeavors believers engage in until the trumpet sounds. In the spiritual sense, being ready involves one major thing which manifests itself in several areas of our lives. If Christians would be ready for Christ, the following areas must be attended to: 1) being born again; 2) manifesting a saving faith in Christ; 3) beginning to show the fruits of the Spirit; 4) desiring greater holiness and less sin in their lives; and 5) consistently looking for His coming.

PRESENT FORBEARANCES THAT FIT WITH CHRIST'S COMPENSATION

Matthew 24:45–47; 1 Peter 5:4; Revelation 3:21; 21:7; 20:4; 2 Timothy 2:12; Daniel 7:17–18; Luke 12:37; Isaiah 32:1

Christ's two counsels above are sacrifices on the part of believers who desire to make heaven a place of abode at all costs. Rather than centering our lives on "eating and drinking, marrying and giving in marriage" (Matthew 24:38), we should be engaging in those spiritual endeavors that are key to believers' reigning with Christ in heaven. In Matthew 24:45–47, Christ says, "Who then is a faithful and wise servant, whom his lord hath made ruler over his household, to give them meat in due season? Blessed is that servant, whom his lord when he cometh shall find so doing. Verily I say unto you, That he shall make him ruler over all his goods." Christ is assuring us that the faithful and wise servants who take heed of His words will earn the reward of ruling and reigning with Christ in the millennial kingdom and in heaven.

Theme

THE PREPARED AND THE UNPREPARED IN THE CHURCH OF GOD

Text(s): Matthew 25:1–13

Lesson Introduction: The parable in Matthew 25:1–13 centers around two distinct groups of believers who are typical of the believers in Christ's church today. Both groups are waiting for the coming of the Lord (the Bridegroom). In this parable, Christ's focus is on His own people, the Brides of Christ (Revelation 21:2, 9). The Brides of Christ are known as virgins. The term *virgin* in the Bible denotes spiritual purity. Also, virginity is often associated with salvation in the Bible, and it shows fidelity to Christ alone (Revelation 14:4). The people outside the church are not spiritually pure, do not clamor for Christ, and have no relationship with Him. Christ comes for the virgins who are ready to receive Him, so that He can take them to heaven; the foolish, unprepared virgins He leaves behind in the world.

BREAKDOWN OF THE STUDY

1. The Careless Ones in the Pursuit of the Bridegroom
2. The Cautious Ones in the Pursuit and Preparations for the Bridegroom
3. Christ's Unapologetic Pronouncements, a Baseline for Comparison

THE CARELESS ONES IN THE PURSUIT OF THE BRIDEGROOM

Matthew 25:1, 3, 6–8, 10; Isaiah 29:13; Ezekiel 33:31;
Acts 8:21; Psalm 78:36–37; Luke 9:62

The parable Christ shared entails those virgins who declared that they believed in Christ and were waiting for His coming. They believed themselves to be die-hard followers of the Bridegroom. However, when the Bridegroom arrived and they were put to the test, they failed. They were found lacking in their preparations and their commitment. The five virgins who were not prepared when the Bridegroom arrived are very much like many current members of the church. They may always be physically present in the church and claim that Christ (the Bridegroom) is always the focus in all of their meetings, but like the five unprepared virgins, their hearts are far from Christ whom they seek in the church. In Matthew 15:8, Christ said "This people draweth nigh unto me with their mouth, and honoureth me with their lips; but their heart is far from me". In our world today, there are people who are regular church attendees but are not truly followers of Christ. They appear to be true followers in their dress and their regular attendance at church services; however, they deny Christ by their conduct.

THE CAUTIOUS ONES IN THE PURSUIT AND PREPARATIONS FOR THE BRIDEGROOM

Matthew 25:1–5, 7–9; 11:12; Philippians 2:12; Luke 16:16;
2 Peter 1:5–10; Luke 13:23–24; Hebrews 4:11; 12:28–29

The difference between the cautious and the careless Christians is the extra effort the cautious Christians demonstrate regularly. In Philippians 2:12, the Bible admonishes believers, "Wherefore, my beloved, as ye have always obeyed, not as in my presence only, but now much more in my absence, work out your own salvation with fear and trembling." The phrase *work out your own salvation with fear and trembling* means that believers should work with careful attentiveness, tenderness of heart, and watchfulness against temptation and regularly come into the presence of the Lord to obtain grace to live day by day for the Lord. In our text, Matthew 25, the wise virgins were watching carefully and putting everything in order in their lives, so that their singular goal of going with the Bridegroom, when He came for them, was achieved.

CHRIST'S UNAPOLOGETIC PRONOUNCEMENTS, A BASELINE FOR COMPARISON

Matthew 25:10–13; Luke 13:26–30; 1 Corinthians 8:13; Hebrews 10:38; 1 Timothy 4:10; John 10:27; 15:2; 6:37; Romans 9:6; 1 John 2:19

Christ was able to easily distinguish between the two groups that were waiting for Him. In Matthew 25:10–13, the Bible states, "And while they went to buy, the Bridegroom came; and they that were ready went in with him to the marriage: and the door was shut." Christ's ultimate yardstick is *readiness*. For example, the five wise virgins had adequate reserves of oil to last them whether the Bridegroom arrived when expected or at a later time. The foolish virgins, on the other hand were "on and off" Brides (meaning that sometimes they would have oil and sometimes not), and unfortunately, they ran out of oil when it was most important.

Christ's description of the five foolish virgins can also apply to those who are anxiously waiting for Him in the Bible. In Matthew 24:13, Christ said, "But he that shall endure unto the end, the same shall be saved." This means that the five foolish virgins could not endure to the end. Finally, Christ's Word says that "no man, having put his hand to the plough, and looking back, is fit for the kingdom of God" (Luke 9:62). By Christ's own words, the five foolish virgins made an error in judgment and therefore were disqualified from the kingdom of God.

Theme

SERVING GOD WITH OUR UNIQUE TALENTS/GIFTS TO THE BEST OF OUR ABILITY

Text(s): Matthew 25:14–30

Lesson Introduction: Christ made frequent use of parables that contained spiritual meanings and were meant to address important subjects. All of His parables were geared toward drawing people to a consciousness of heaven. In Matthew 25:14–30, Christ's parable tells us about a man placing his goods in the care of three of his servants. In our chosen text, *goods* means talents, money, and gifts. Like the master in this story, God dispenses gifts and talents on the basis of an individual's abilities. God dispenses His gifts and talents to all men and women to further the kingdom of God. The gifts and talents that God gives to everyone are diverse, with each one being important to Him. God rewards those who use their gifts and talents to the maximum; He condemns those who, through lack of faith, fail to use the gifts and talents with which He has graced them.

BREAKDOWN OF THE STUDY

1. Gifts Distributed in Proper Proportion
2. Gifts Determined on Personal Potential
3. God's Declarations on Productivity of His Servants

GIFTS DISTRIBUTED IN PROPER PROPORTION

Matthew 25:14–15; Ephesians 4:8; 1 Peter 4:10; 1
Corinthians 7:7; 12:4, 8; 1 Kings 3:12; Acts 19:8

This parable addresses how valuable and important human beings are to
God. God has endowed each and every one of us with unique gifts and
talents. This parable was delivered to Christ's followers, His servants.
Because they believed that Christ was the Son of the living God, it was
important for them to understand that God had graced them with gifts
and talents so that they might be productive. The master in this parable
granted each servant responsibility in proportion to his ability. God does
the same with us. And it is important to note that while God, in His
discretion, grants different gifts and talents to each individual, it is obvious
that God has blessed every one of us with at least one gift or talent. He has
blessed some people with more than one gift or talent. Therefore, there
is no one who has a relationship with Christ, who has not been given a
minimum talent or gift to be used for God.

GIFTS DETERMINED ON PERSONAL POTENTIAL

Matthew 25:14–15; Romans 12:3–9; James 4:6; Ephesians
4:7–13; 1 Corinthians 12:7–11; John 3:34; Galatians
2:8–9

In this parable Christ points out that the master of the house used his
discretion in determining how much to give each servant, based on the
servant's demonstrated potential. One servant was not deemed to be
better than the other; all of them were worthy servants and disciples.
However, the master distributed his wealth among his servants based on
each one's skills and abilities. He expected each one to capitalize on his
own unique abilities. In Matthew 25:14–15, Christ shows us that, while
people are uniquely qualified, no one is better than another. Likewise,
God's expectations of His servants vary just as their ability levels vary.
Therefore, everyone who is a servant must make judicious use of their
gift(s). In Romans 12:3–9, the Bible cautions servants not to feel they are

superior to others because of their gifts; everyone working for Christ has different offices. God bestows His gifts on the basis of grace; therefore, every one of us must be diligent in the office we have been endowed to minister, whether in prophecy, in teaching, in exhortation, in cheerfulness, in giving, or in the demonstration of love.

GOD'S DECLARATIONS ON PRODUCTIVITY OF HIS SERVANTS

Matthew 25:16–30; 16:27; Luke 19:17; 1 Corinthians 3:14–15; 3:8; 4:5; Numbers 12:7; Hebrews 3:2–6

Christ's parables have spiritual interpretations and serve as lessons to His servants and disciples. In Matthew 25:16, the first two servants were thoughtful about the gifts and talents given to them by their master. The moment their master left them for a journey, the first two servants, who received the most based upon their demonstrated abilities, rose up to action. The two servants with the most ability became productive and gained greater wealth for their master. They proved that they were deserving of the confidence their master had in them. The third man, the one with the least ability, underestimated the worth of his gift or talent and failed to be productive. He wasted his unique talent. The moral of the parable is that the master recognized the efforts of the two industrious servants and rewarded them with greater responsibilities and greater joy. However, the third man was chastised for his lack of faith and lost all that he possessed. Each servant was treated justly by his master, the same as we will be treated justly by God.

Theme

MANDATORY RESPONSIBILITIES EXPECTED OF CHRIST'S DISCIPLES

Text(s): Matthew 25:31–46; Hebrews 13:16; 1 Timothy 6:17–19

Lesson Introduction: The judgment that Christ speaks about in Matthew 25:31–46 is directed to His disciples. Christ is revealing the mandated responsibilities His disciples have to the people in the church, to those outside the church, and to those who are imprisoned for their irresponsible acts. A thorough understanding of Christ's mission of compassion and love must compel all His true disciples to reach out to those who do not know Christ. This text speaks to the fact that Christ's true disciples possess a good understanding of their expected responsibilities and that they will be judged on how well they carry out those responsibilities. In James 4:17, the Bible states: "To him that knoweth to do good, and doeth it not, to him it is sin." Christ's disciples will be judged on their sins of *omission* as well as their sins of *commission.*

BREAKDOWN OF THE STUDY

1. Ministering to the Wretched in the Church
2. Ministering to the Wanderers outside the Church
3. Maintaining Workable Outreach to the Confined and the Sick

MINISTERING TO THE WRETCHED
IN THE CHURCH

Matthew 25:35, 42; 1 John 3:16–19; Deuteronomy 15:7–11; James 2:15–16; Romans 12:13; 1 Peter 4:9–10; Hebrews 6:10; Philemon 1:7; Acts 11:29

Christ's message to Christians is to consider the wretched among them and show love to the brethren in the church (Matthew 25:40). In Matthew 25:34–35, Christ commended His disciples who met the needs of others, saying, "For I was an hungred, and ye gave me meat: I was thirsty, and ye gave me drink." The Lord ushered them into His kingdom by saying "Then shall the King say unto them on his right hand, come ye blessed of my Father, inherit the kingdom prepared for you from the foundation of the world" (Matthew 25:34). Likewise, Christ chastised those Christians who never showed love and compassion to those who were around them and with them in the Church. He said, "For I was an hungred, and ye gave me no meat: I was thirsty, and ye gave me no drink" (Matthew 25:42). The important lesson is that Christians need to minister to the needy among them.

MINISTERING TO THE WANDERERS
OUTSIDE THE CHURCH

Matthew 25:35, 43; Ezekiel 18:7, 16; Job 31:32; Romans 16:23; 12:20; Hebrews 13:1–3; 3 John 1:5–8; Acts 16:15; Luke 14:12–14; Proverbs 14:31

Christ also admonishes Christians to care for strangers. The strangers among us may be homeless people who wander from place to place. They may come from other communities or other cultures. They may need a lot of help to assimilate into the local community. Christ warns His followers that they will be judged by how well they receive strangers. In Matthew 25:35, Christ said to the brethren, "I was a stranger, and ye took me in." Christians must care for all of their fellow human beings, not only their relatives, friends, fellow church members, or Christian brethren. Failure to care for strangers is failure to care for Christ. "I was a stranger, and ye took me not in: naked and ye clothed me not" (Matthew 25:43).

MAINTAINING WORKABLE OUTREACH TO THE CONFINED AND THE SICK

> Matthew 25:36, 43; John 5:1–8; Acts 9:36; Hebrews 13:3; 10:34; 2 Timothy 1:16–18; Luke 10:36; James 1:27

Christ's message to His church involves ministering to all of His people and not only the righteous in the church or the strangers in our neighborhoods. Christ's disciples are called to go out and feed the hungry, provide drink to the thirsty, welcome the stranger, and visit the sick and those who are imprisoned or confined. Christ's disciples must reach out, with love and compassion, not only to our Christian brothers and sisters, but to all those in need. In Matthew 25:34–36, Christ commended those Christians who were dutiful in reaching out to the sick and the confined or imprisoned. But the Christians who neglected to visit the sick and imprisoned did not receive the favor of the Lord (Matthew 25:45–46).

Theme

REVELATIONS ABOUT CHRIST BEING THE SACRIFICE FOR SINS

Text(s): Matthew 26:1–5, 14, 24, 26–28

Lesson Introduction: "In the mouth of two or three witnesses shall every word be established" (2 Corinthians 13:1). The truth about Christ being the Sacrifice for our sins is confirmed by the religious leaders and by Christ Himself. Caiaphas, being the high priest, prophesied that Jesus should die for that nation (John 11:51). In Matthew 26:28, Christ declares that "this is my blood of the new testament, which is shed for many for the remission of sins." Christ's words inform everyone of the importance of accepting Christ as the Begotten of the Father and the only acceptable One through which forgiveness will be earned (John 1:14). The apostle Peter, filled with the Holy Ghost, declared in Acts 4:12 that "neither is there salvation in any other, for there is none other name under heaven given among men, whereby we must be saved." Christ is the only hope for anyone under the New Testament dispensation. He is central to earning salvation and being able to live with God in Heaven.

BREAKDOWN OF THE STUDY

1. Christ's Prediction of His Crucifixion
2. Consultation and Plans to Crucify Christ
3. Christ, the Promised Sin Bearer

CHRIST'S PREDICTION OF HIS CRUCIFIXION

Matthew 26:1–2; Psalm 22:16; Zechariah 12:10; Isaiah 53:5

Christ predicted His crucifixion before He was taken by the religious leaders (Matthew 26:2). Christ knew that the Scriptures must be fulfilled concerning His death on the cross. According to Matthew 26:54, Christ said, "But how then shall the scriptures be fulfilled, that thus it must be?" Therefore, Christ came into the world to fulfill all those things the prophets of old had said about Him. Christ could, on His own, subvert the plans of God but decided the will of God for Him must be fulfilled (Matthew 26:39). In addition, the crucifixion of Christ was revealed in the Old Testament. In Psalm 22:16, the Lord (Messiah) had in mind how the Roman soldiers laid rough hands on Him and pierced His hands and feet (Matthew 27:27-35).

CONSULTATION AND PLANS TO CRUCIFY CHRIST

Matthew 26:3–5, 14; Psalm 94:20–21; 64:4–6; Acts 4:25–28; John 18:13–15

Matthew 26:3–5 reveals the scheme of the religious leaders (chief priests, scribes, and elders of the people) coming together to complete their plans for arresting Christ and eventually crucifying Him. Also, the Old Testament reveals the plans of the wicked for the fulfillment of God's plan. In Psalm 94:20–21, the Bible declares, "Shall the throne of iniquity have fellowship with thee, which frameth mischief by a law? They gather themselves together against the soul of the righteous, and condemn the innocent blood." Those religious leaders in Matthew 26:3–5 could not find fault or any reasons to condemn Christ, but, through mischief and false witnesses, they were able to justify why He should die on the cross (Matthew 26:59–61).

CHRIST, THE PROMISED SIN BEARER

Matthew 26:24, 26–28; Luke 2:10–11; 4:16–21; 24:47; Romans 6:23; Hebrews 9:28; 1 Peter 2:24; 1 John 3:5; Micah 5:2

Christ came to fulfil all that was written about Him, including dying on the cross of Calvary, to be the final Sin Bearer of the New Testament believers. In Matthew 26:24, 26–28, Christ declares that He came into the world to offer His blood "which is shed for many for the remission of sins." Our heavenly Father (God) testified of His beloved Son to Christ's disciples: "While he [Peter] yet spake, behold, a bright cloud overshadowed them: and behold a voice out of the cloud, which said, this is my beloved Son, in whom I am well pleased; hear ye him" (Matthew 17:5). God is well pleased with the Son, and He stands by every word Christ said about Himself being the reparation for the sins of the world. Christ is the light, the life and the hope of the world; it is through Christ that a sinner is saved and receives increased hope for eternal life (John 1:1–9; Romans 5:3–5). The promise of living with Christ in heaven gives a believer in Christ a determination to endure life's trials.

Theme

RESOLVING TO PRAY IN DIFFICULT MOMENTS

Text(s): Matthew 26:1–4, 18, 20–29, 31–36, 54–56, 64

Lesson Introduction: Christ approached His death in a way very different from how ordinary people would have handled it. Ordinary people would fight for their lives, seek help from the courts of law, and spend a lot of money to avert a death sentence. However, Christ's approach at this crucial time of His life was to go to God in prayer (Matthew 26:36–42). Christ was resigned to His death and spoke about it with His disciples. Even the religious leaders of the day knew that Christ had to die (Matthew 26:3–4). Therefore, Christ did not resort to asking His disciples about how He might escape to another city. In order to fulfill the prophecies recorded in the Scriptures, He was ready to face death (Matthew 26:54–56). Christ's method of handling this challenge should be a model to be followed by Christians today. Challenges come in different forms: unfavorable living conditions, false allegations, and even terminal illnesses. All can be handled with prayer.

BREAKDOWN OF THE STUDY

1. Christ's Concerns before Prayer
2. Christ's Comfort during Prayer
3. Christ's Confidence after Prayer

CHRIST'S CONCERNS BEFORE PRAYER

Matthew 26:1–4, 18, 20–29, 31–38, 45; Acts 18:9; Jonah 3:4; 2 Chronicles 20:1–3; 2 Chronicles 33:12; Isaiah 38:1

Christ spoke about being betrayed by His own chosen disciple, which would eventually lead to His death. Christ, as a man, was troubled and feared for His life. In Matthew 26:2, Christ shared with His disciples, "Ye know that after two days is the feast of the passover, and the Son of man is betrayed to be crucified." Christ's disciples understood the word *crucified*, which means to be nailed or bound to a cross to die. Once again, in Matthew 26:20–29, Christ states that he will be betrayed by one of his own. This truth brought great sorrow to His disciples. In verses 31–38, Christ demonstrated His own sorrow that His disciples would abandon Him by denying they ever had a relationship with Him. It definitely hurts to know that those you have lived and shared your life with would abandon you when you need them most.

CHRIST'S COMFORT DURING PRAYER

Matthew 26:36–44; John 12:27–30; Acts 7:56; 18:9–10; 2 Timothy 4:17

Christ had the strength and the grace not to allow the reality that His disciples would deny Him to weigh down His spirit. Rather, He mustered the courage to do what He had always done: to seek God in prayer. Matthew 26:36–45 tells us that Christ, during this dark time in His life, took all of His disciples to a place called Gethsemane in order to pray for God's divine intervention. Christ prayed on his own behalf and sought the prayers of His closest disciples (Peter, James, and John). He had hoped that His disciples would share His burden, but when Christ needed them the most, they could not even stay awake. Nonetheless, because Christ spent quality time with God in prayer, He was comforted and received the inner strength to deal with death.

CHRIST'S CONFIDENCE AFTER PRAYER

Matthew 26:45–56, 64; 14:23; Hebrews 5:7; Luke 3:21; 6:12; Mark 1:35; Isaiah 53:12

Christ's attitude toward those who came to arrest Him demonstrated that He believed in the power of prayer. Christ said to them, "Thinkest thou that I cannot now pray to my Father and he shall presently give me more than twelve legions of angels? But how then shall the scriptures be fulfilled, that thus it must be?" (Matthew 26:53–54). Christ knew that if He asked in prayer, His Father could send legions of angels to fight for Him in His time of need. Doing so, however, would prevent the Scriptures concerning his mission from being fulfilled. Christ had to die for the sins of the world. That was the very reason He had come into the world. By His actions, Christ informs Christians that when we pray in the face of life's challenges, God will prevail for us. Divine help will be available in all the circumstances of our lives. In verse 64 of Matthew 26, Christ revealed to the chief priests, elders, and all the council the confidence He had in His Father's ultimate answer to His prayers, when He stated, "Hereafter shall ye see the Son of man sitting on the right hand of power, and coming in the clouds of heaven."

Theme

FULFILLING THE COMPLETE SCRIPTURES WITHOUT MODIFICATIONS

Text(s): Matthew 26: 24, 31, 41, 54, 56

Lesson Introduction: Christ came to fulfill the written Word of God. He did not modify the Scriptures to avoid fulfilling His purpose on earth. Like Christ, we need to follow the Scriptures without reservation. The Scriptures are the inspired Word of God. They are to be followed in their entirety, with nothing added and nothing deleted. Christ came to fulfill the Old Testament prophecies, as given by God to the prophets of old. Because He understood the need to follow the will of God, Christ turned to prayer for the strength to do His Father's will. He did not attempt to avoid or alter it. As Christians, we are called to follow Christ's example. We need to pray for the courage to listen to and obey the Word of God.

BREAKDOWN OF THE STUDY

1. The Written Word
2. Working within the Written Word
3. Willingness to Work the Written Word through Prayer

THE WRITTEN WORD

Matthew 26:24, 31, 54; 56; 4:4, 6–7, 10; Luke 4:4; Romans 15:4; 1 Corinthians 10:11; 2 Timothy 3:16–17; 1 Corinthians 9:9–10

The written Word of God has the final say in all matters as it relates to us; it cannot be modified or changed to suit our needs but must be followed to the letter. The written Word of God is relevant in all dispensations. The first five books of the Bible (Genesis, Exodus, Leviticus, Numbers, and Deuteronomy) were passed down orally by God to Moses, who put them into writing for the children of Israel to follow. The remaining thirty-four books of the Old Testament were written by the prophets of old and other designated persons. These thirty-nine books are the inspired and unadulterated Word of God. In Matthew 26:54, 56, Christ said, "But how then shall the scriptures be fulfilled, that thus it must be? … But all this was done, that the scriptures of the prophets might be fulfilled." Christ's statement reaffirms that the Old Testament is the unadulterated, infallible and unchanging written Word of God for all times.

WORKING WITHIN THE WRITTEN WORD

Matthew 26:54, 56; 5:17–19; Acts 1:16–23; 2:23; Revelation 1:9; 6:9 Luke 16:17; 24:24

The Scriptures (both the Old and New Testaments) are given to Christians as a complete manual to be followed. The Scriptures are a guide for our spiritual journey on Earth. The word *BIBLE* may be taken as an acronym for ***B**asic **I**nstructions **B**efore **L**eaving **E**arth*. In Matthew 26:54, 56, Christ explained that He came not to do His own will, but that of His heavenly Father. Christ accepted God's will as declared in the Old Testament, that He should go to the cross and die for humanity. Christ aligned His will to the Father's will.

Christ's attitude toward the Scriptures is a model for all believers in the New Testament dispensation. In Matthew 5:17–18, Christ states, "Think not that I am come to destroy the law, or the prophets: I am not come to destroy, but to fulfil. For verily I say unto you, till heaven and earth pass, one jot or one tittle shall in no wise pass from the law, till all be fulfilled." Christ modeled for His believers the importance of studying the Word of God and working out its meaning in our lives.

WILLINGNESS TO WORK THE WRITTEN WORD THROUGH PRAYER

Matthew 26:41; 4:1–4; Acts 4:31; 13:2–3; Daniel 6:5, 7, 10

Christ knew what was written in the Word of God about how He was to die on the cross. He understood that was His mission, the reason He came into the world. Nonetheless, as a man, Christ feared the prospect of His pending death (Matthew 26:39, 42, 44). Yet He concluded that the will of the Father must be done and voluntarily yielded Himself to death. It was the quality time He spent before God that prepared Him for the death that He was about to suffer. He prayed for the strength to accept His fate. He also encouraged His disciples to pray. In Matthew 26:41, Christ told His disciples, "Watch and pray, that ye enter not into temptation: the spirit indeed is willing, but the flesh is weak." The importance of prayer in reaching a decision to obey God's written Word cannot be overemphasized. It is through prayer that the inner man is strengthened to obey God in all circumstances. The temptation Christ spoke about to His disciples, has the potential to thwart anyone from following the written Word of God. For example, all the disciples denied Christ at the time when He needed their support the most. It is critical for us to be prayerful in challenging times, in order not to deny Christ. In Matthew 10:33, Christ states, "But whosoever shall deny me before men, him will I also deny before my Father which is heaven."

FORFEITING GODLY SALVATION AFTER REPENTANCE

Text(s): Matthew 27:1–5

Lesson Introduction: When Judas Iscariot realized he had been instrumental in the condemnation of Christ, he regretted his sinfulness in having betrayed an innocent person. He showed his remorse in two ways: First, Judas lamented betraying the innocent Christ. Second, Judas refused to keep the money that was given to him. Judas Iscariot's actions follow biblical teachings on *repentance and restitution* (see Leviticus 6:2–5; Numbers 5:6–7). Nonetheless, his decision to take his own life, by hanging himself, has been frowned upon by many theologians and conservative Christians. Early church councils denied Christian burial to those guilty of suicide. In summary, suicide is forbidden and deemed as unacceptable in Christendom, regardless of life's misfortunes.

BREAKDOWN OF THE STUDY

1. Descriptions of Genuine Repentance
2. Demonstrations of Genuine Repentance
3. Denunciation of Gross Misrepresentation of Beliefs

DESCRIPTIONS OF GENUINE REPENTANCE

Matthew 27:1–4; 3:6; Luke 19:1–7; 5:8–9; 3:8; 15:17–18;
1 John 1:19; Romans 10:10; Psalm 32:5; 2 Samuel 12:13;
2 Corinthians 7:10; Isaiah 6:5

Judas Iscariot, without being faulted by anyone, but pricked in his heart, declared himself a sinner. He had a genuine repentance, and he was remorseful for his nefarious act (Matthew 27:1–4). His suicidal act was not premeditated; it was an impulsive response to having witnessed what was done to Christ. Judas Iscariot's experience is similar to that of Zacchaeus, as cited in Luke 19:1–7. Zacchaeus was the chief tax collector, and it was then common knowledge that tax collectors got wealthy by cheating others. Therefore, Zacchaeus was not qualified to receive Jesus as a guest in his house. The crowd that was with Jesus referred to Zacchaeus as a sinner, and Zacchaeus did not refute the allegation. In summary, a recipient of genuine salvation is not ashamed of accepting guilt in the midst of a crowd.

DEMONSTRATION OF GENUINE REPENTANCE

Matthew 27:3–5; Luke 19:8; Acts 19:18–19; Ezra 10:1;
Numbers 5:6–7; Proverbs 6:31; Exodus 22:2–3, 7;
Leviticus 6:2–5; Romans 10:10

Judas Iscariot demonstrated genuine repentance by confessing his sin to the elders and returning the bounty he had received for betraying Christ. Most likely, Judas had knowledge of the Old Testament or had heard Christ teach about repentance and restitution. In Matthew 27:3–4, the Scripture declares, "Then Judas, which had betrayed him, when he saw that he was condemned, repented himself, and brought again the thirty pieces of silver to the chief priests and elders, saying, I have sinned in that I have betrayed the innocent blood. And they said, What is that to us? see thou to that." Judas's motive for betraying Christ was to profit financially. He may have originally thought that revealing Christ's identity was not a big deal, but when his actions resulted in Christ being put to death, Judas was filled with regret. He demonstrated the level of his repentance when he brought the pieces of silver to the chief priests and elders "and cast down the pieces of silver in the temple" (Matthew 27:5). The depth of Judas's contrition was evident in returning his ill-gotten gain. The love of God moves a repentant sinner to make restitution both in word and in amended actions

DENUNCIATION OF GROSS MISREPRESENTATION OF BELIEFS

Matthew 27:5; Acts 18:5–6; 4:12; Joshua 24:15; John 6:67–68; Exodus 23:24

Judas Iscariot's action, as a disciple of Christ, contradicts the teachings of Christ in the New Testament. Judas Iscariot had forgotten the teachings of Christ on coping and handling life's challenges. He threw out of the window his genuine acts of repentance and restitution and chose to kill himself. His own confession condemned him, as he referred to himself as a sinner; he carried a condemned heart to his grave. In 1 John 3:20, the Bible states that "if our heart condemn us, God is greater than our heart, and knoweth all things." Therefore, Judas Iscariot understood the Scriptures that say, "All unrighteousness is sin" (1 John 5:17). Peter's narrative of Judas Iscariot in the Upper Room was not complimentary either; rather, it portrayed Judas as a despicable man and an outcast from Christ's ministry. Thus the cogent reason for his replacement in the group (Psalm 109:8; Acts 1:20).

Some theologians believe Judas Iscariot's suicidal act has nothing to do with his salvation. In other words, Judas Iscariot still had his salvation experience. Accepting this claim only promotes the doctrine of "once saved is saved forever," regardless of what a believer does with his or her life. Such teaching is not scriptural. Sin committed after a repentance experience disqualifies one from being a child of God, *if not confessed.* Many scriptures clearly denounce unrighteous acts after salvation (Ezekiel 33:18; Hebrews 3:6, 12–14; Matthew 24:13; 1 Corinthians 1:8; Revelation 2:10).

PREVAILING IN THE
MIDST OF OPPOSITION

Text(s): Matthew 26:36–44; 27:11–14

Lesson Introduction: When it comes to the difficult circumstances of life, Christians' attitudes must be different from non-Christians. According to the Scriptures, "A good tree bringeth not forth corrupt fruit, neither doth a corrupt tree bring forth good fruit. For every tree is known by his own fruit …. A good man out of the good treasure of his heart bringeth forth that which is good" (Luke 6:43–45). Christians are the redeemed of the Lord. As followers of Christ, Christians must remain in control of themselves, act properly, and glorify the name of God at all times. Christ, during His three years and six months of public ministry, faced opposition from many of the religious leaders. Christ persevered despite their fierce criticism because He prayed daily for victory over His critics. As an example for all Christians, Christ never wavered before those who tried to incriminate and get rid of Him. He prevailed over His accusers and emerged as a just man.

BREAKDOWN OF THE STUDY

1. Prevailing Prayer for Proper Character
2. Proper Proclamations under the Pressure of Persecutors
3. Posture of Persevering Pilgrim

PREVAILING PRAYER FOR PROPER CHARACTER

Matthew 26:36–44; 14:23; Luke 6:12; Mark 6:46;
Hebrews 5:7; Colossians 4:2; Daniel 6:10; Psalm 109:3–4

Christ came into the world to teach us how to seek His heavenly Father. Jesus demonstrated the importance of prayer when He began each morning by withdrawing to pray (Mark 1:35–36). By witnessing how Christ lived a prayerful life, His disciples and followers learned the value that the Lord placed on prayer. As Christ accepted that His hour of death was approaching, He went to the garden of Gethsemane. There, He prayed for the strength to bear the weight of the fate that awaited Him (Matthew 26:36–44). Christ was able to face those who would falsely accuse Him and crucify Him because He was strengthened by prayer. The importance of the role that prayer plays in the life of a Christian cannot be overemphasized. In all circumstances, prayer has the power to humble and strengthen Christians and align their will to the will of God.

PROPER PROCLAMATIONS UNDER THE PRESSURE OF PERSECUTORS

Matthew 26:63–64; 27:11; 1 Timothy 6:13; Luke 23:2–3;
John 18:36–37; 19:11; Acts 4:31, 33

Christ did not fail God by denying His relationship with God to escape death. Having been prepared through prayer, Christ humbled Himself before the religious leaders, even though doing so gave them ammunition to use against Him. When Christ was questioned by the high priest about being "the Christ, the Son of God," He replied by saying, "Thou hast said" (Matthew 26:63–64). Also, in Matthew 27:11, we read that "Jesus stood before the governor: and the governor asked him, saying, Art thou the king of the Jews? And Jesus said unto him, Thou sayest." In this, Christ provided the religious leaders with the sound bite that they would use against Him. Throughout His trials and eventual condemnation, the religious leaders and soldiers referenced Christ as saying that He called Himself "the Son of God and the King of the Jews" (Matthew 27:29,

37, 40–42). Again, it was because of His hours of praying to God, that Christ found the strength to declare His identity. Perhaps if Peter and the other disciples had been able to stay awake and pray as Christ had asked (Matthew 26:41), they would have found the courage not to deny Him.

POSTURE OF PERSEVERING PILGRIM

> Matthew 27:12–14; 26:61–63; Colossians 4:12; Luke 21:36; Acts 16:22–25; Daniel 3:12–18; 6:7–10

On the night He was betrayed, Christ prayed to know His Father's will for Him. Having accepted His Father's will, He knew there was nothing to be gained by arguing with the religious leaders or defending Himself against the allegations they levied against Him.

In Ephesians 6:13, the Bible says, "and having done all, to stand." In other words, anyone, having prayed to God, need only wait to experience God's power in action. In Matthew 27:12–14, Pilate, the governor, marveled that Christ did not defend Himself from the accusations brought against Him. He maintained perfect composure and was unruffled by their lies, because He knew that God, and not man, had the final say concerning all things. It is important for Christians to follow Christ's example when facing the issues of this world. After all, Christ was the ultimate victor when His accusers and fault finders later proclaimed Him to be both a just man and the Son of God (Matthew 27:19, 24, 54).

Theme

EXCEPTIONAL FAITHFULNESS GETS GOD'S ATTENTION

Text(s): Matthew 27:55–56, 61; 28:1–7

Lesson Introduction: Many of Christ's closest followers were women, and unlike His disciples, they never abandoned or denied Him. Their love of the Lord was pure and steadfast. Some of those same women were the first to learn of Christ's resurrection. Today, most preachers of the gospel of Christ speak positively about the uniqueness of these women and praise their fidelity to the Lord.

Nonetheless, this lesson transcends a singular focus on a particular gender; rather, our attention is drawn to the call for faithfulness in service by *all* true followers of Christ. In Galatians 3:28, the Bible tells us that "there is neither Jew nor Greek, there is neither bond nor free, *there is neither male nor female: for ye are all one in Christ Jesus*" (emphasis added). Students of the Bible understand that both faithful men and faithful women have demonstrated extraordinary love for God. God acknowledged those people by rewarding their faithfulness in the most unbelievable ways. In our own dispensation, our Lord, Jesus Christ, has been proving Himself to be "the same yesterday and today and forever" in all His divine manifestations among faithful followers (Hebrews 13:8 ESV).

BREAKDOWN OF THE STUDY

1. Faithfulness in Christ's Presence
2. Faithfulness in Christ's Absence
3. Faithfulness Fulfilled of Christ's Precious Followers

FAITHFULNESS IN CHRIST'S PRESENCE

Matthew 27:55–56, 61; 26:17–19; 17:24–27; Luke 9:1–2, 52; 10:1; Mark 12:41–44; Luke 19:8–10

Christ chose twelve male disciples as His core followers to support Him throughout His three years and six months in public ministry on earth. All of them loved and stood by Christ in the good times. However, each of them deserted Christ in His greatest hour of need. Christ also had a cohort of female disciples who accompanied Him throughout His public ministry. They were faithful to Him even during His trial and crucifixion. These women were very dear to Christ, because of their faithfulness to Him. Mary Magdalene, the woman Christ delivered from seven demons (Mark 16:9), showed unwavering faithfulness to Christ during His ordeal with the religious leaders. All four of the Gospel writers (Matthew, Mark, Luke, and John) mention the name of Mary Magdalene before listing the names of the other women in His cohort of followers. These women ministered to Christ when He was alive and were sitting over against His sepulcher (Matthew 27:61; Mark 16:9; Luke 24:10; John 20:18). Their service to Christ poses a serious challenge to us today.

FAITHFULNESS IN CHRIST'S ABSENCE

Matthew 28:1; Acts 4:5–20; 5:25–29; Daniel 6:10; 1 Kings 22:14; 1 Thessalonians 2:4; Ephesians 6:6; Galatians 1:10

Matthew, Mark, Luke, and John record that Mary Magdalene and many other women stood with Christ through his trial, crucifixion, and death. They were also the first to discover that He had been raised from the dead

(Mathew 27:55–56, 61; 28:1). The motivation for Mary Magdalene and the other women was not to impress others; rather, their motives were pure and altruistic. They were faithful followers of Christ who genuinely and lovingly wanted to serve the Lord. There are many people who live their lives to impress others so as to gain the favor of the rich and powerful. The fact that Mary Magdalene and the other women mentioned in the Bible remained faithful to Christ even after His death and resurrection proves that they were not driven by social pressure to be faithful to Christ.

FAITHFULNESS FULFILLED OF CHRIST'S PRECIOUS FOLLOWERS

Matthew 28:2–7; Daniel 3:8–25; 6:5–22; Acts 16:16–26; 12:1–10

The relationship between God and His followers is very personal. Mary Magdalene and Christ's other faithful female followers proved this to be true. Their faithfulness was rooted in their personal commitment to Christ, not in seeking the approval of others. God searched the hearts of these women and found that they had a sincere desire to know Jesus. God rewarded the women's dedication by allowing them to be the first witnesses to Christ's resurrection. As reported in Matthew 28:2–7, God sent His angel to the women, who had come to the sepulcher where Christ had been laid, to deliver the good news that Christ had risen from the dead. They were the first believers to witness the fulfillment of God's promise that, though Christ would die, He would rise from the tomb on the third day (Easter Sunday). It cannot be overemphasized that, even today, God richly blesses those who are committed to serving Him fully and faithfully.

THE RISEN CHRIST'S WORDS
TO HIS DISCIPLES

Text(s): Matthew 28:18–20

Lesson Introduction: During Christ's earthly ministry, His disciples believed that He was the Son of God come down from heaven. Even before His death, crucifixion, and resurrection, His disciples recognized Him as Lord. Immediately after Christ's resurrection, His disciples (Mary Magdalene, other women, and some of His eleven followers) saw Him as the glorified Lord because they now worshipped Him unreservedly (Matthew 28:9, 17). This demonstration of reverence for Christ by the disciples soon became a new way to approach Christ and see Him. The risen Lord is now Lord of all, who has control over everything, both on earth and in heaven. The disciples realized that Christ is omnipotent, omniscient, and omnipresent. As the glorified Lord, empowered by the God of heaven, He commissioned His disciples to make disciples for Him in the world. Christ has given assurances of His power and presence to His disciples throughout the world.

BREAKDOWN OF THE STUDY

1. The Power of Christ in the World
2. Performing Christ's Words in the World
3. The Presence of Christ with the Called-Out Disciples in the World

THE POWER OF CHRIST IN THE WORLD

Matthew 28:18; Acts 3:1–6, 16; 10:38; 4:10; 9:34; 16:18;
Mark 16:17; 2 Corinthians 8:9; 1 Peter 3:22; Ephesians
1:20–22; Daniel 7:13–14; 1 Corinthians 15:27

The triumphant living Christ comes to His disciples, informing them that He possesses power to run the affairs of heaven and earth (Matthew 28:18). Christ's emphasis on *power* to His disciples is necessary in order for them to know that they have Him backing them up every step of the way in their assignment. Christ's power is what the disciples need to overcome all physical and spiritual challenges to their proclaiming the gospel throughout all the world. In Matthew 28:18, Christ says: "All power is given unto me in heaven and in earth." Christ's *power* is in His name, *Jesus*. After Christ's final ascension to heaven, His disciples used His name at different times for divine intervention. In Acts 3:1–6, Peter and John proclaimed the power of Christ when they interjected "the name of Jesus Christ of Nazareth" to heal a certain man that was lame from his mother's womb. *The name of Jesus* is the *power* that Christ has given to His disciples today. Let's use the name of *Jesus* for wonders in our world.

PERFORMING CHRIST'S WORDS IN THE WORLD

Matthew 28:19; Acts 15:35; 11:19; 8:4; 28:31; 1
Thessalonians 2:2; Colossians 1:28

The Word of the Lord for His disciples is to "go ye therefore, and teach all nations, baptizing them in the name of the Father, and of the Son, and of the Holy Ghost: teaching them to observe all things whatsoever I have commanded you" (Matthew 28:19–20). The disciples of Christ are to teach *repentance* and *remission of sins* among all nations in the name of Jesus (Luke 24:47). After teachings on repentance and remission of sins, His disciples must baptize those who respond to the calls of genuine repentance. In verse 20 of Matthew 28, Christ indicates that His disciples must teach everything He has commanded them. Teaching is different than preaching. To preach is to give advice on morality or behavior to others. Christ expects His disciples to teach repentance and remission of sins (Luke 24:47). Having taught the nations, the disciples are to baptize them "in the name of the Father, and of the Son, and of the Holy Ghost" (Matthew 28:19).

THE PRESENCE OF CHRIST WITH THE CALLED-OUT DISCIPLES IN THE WORLD

Matthew 28:20; Isaiah 41:10; Genesis 39:21; Exodus 3:12; Joshua 1:5; John 14:18–23; Mark 16:20; 2 Timothy 4:17

The closing promise of Christ of His ever-presence with the disciples transcends the eleven disciples with Him at that time. His presence is also for those that would come after the first chosen disciples. Christ gives His word to the disciples in order for them not to fear for their lives as a result of threats from their adversaries. In Psalm 138:2, the psalmist indicates of the Lord: "thou hast magnified thy word above all thy name." The Word of the Lord can be trusted, and Christ's disciples can forge on in obeying the commandments of the Lord always. After Christ's final ascension to heaven, the disciples faced oppositions from religious leaders and those people that Satan sent their way. But Christ's presence in those circumstances set them free. In Acts 18:9–10, the Lord spoke to Paul in a vision not to be afraid, but to continue to speak with the people and not be silent because He was with Paul, and nobody would be able to attack him in order to harm him.

FOLLOWING THE TEMPLATE OF HEAVEN ON EARTH

Text(s): Matthew 28:2–10

Lesson Introduction: For any organization to succeed, its underlying philosophy must be understood, believed, and pursued collectively. Each individual contributes to the success of the whole by carrying out their role to the best of their abilities. Therefore, every role is critical to achieving success; no part is less important than any other. An organization that minimizes or neglects any of its component parts risks failing to execute its mission. Successful organizations operate as a team, with each member carrying out their assigned responsibilities. Teamwork requires unanimity, team spirit, and the collective energy of the group. Everyone is called upon to sacrifice for the greater good of the organization. One acronym for "team" is "**T**ogether **E**veryone **A**chieves **M**ore."

BREAKDOWN OF THE STUDY

1. Common Goals
2. Concentration on a Concrete Goal
3. Coalescing behind a Common Goal

COMMON GOALS

Matthew 28:2–10, 18–20; Mark 15:40; John 19:25; Exodus 4:14, 27; Genesis 11:1–3; Exodus 2:3–10; Acts 1:13–15; 2:1

The narrative found in Matthew 28:2–10 reveals that each character—God, Jesus, the angel, Mary Magdalene, and the other women—had a specific role in revealing Christ's resurrection. The well-formed plan called for a particular angel to be present to meet with Mary Magdalene and the other women when they arrived at the place where Jesus had been buried. The angel announced that Christ was risen and instructed them to go and tell the other disciples. As they did the angel's bidding, Christ appeared to them, confirming that He had, indeed, risen from the dead. He affirmed that they were to tell the other disciples of the resurrection and instruct them to go to Galilee. The revelation of Christ's resurrection relied on each character in this story carrying out their assigned responsibility. While Christ is of higher rank than the angel; and the angel is of greater rank than Mary Magdalene and the other women, nonetheless, only by their working together was God's plan properly completed. The lesson for organizations and establishments on earth is that God's plan for humanity will only be realized when we work together as a team

CONCENTRATION ON A CONCRETE GOAL

Matthew 28:2–7; Mark 1:3–4, 6–8, 9–11; Acts 15:35; 8:5, 14; Luke 10:1; 1:11–17, 19, 26–33; Isaiah 38:1, 5; Mark 16:1

There is an obvious hierarchy in this story. It cannot be overemphasized that the angel is less than Christ in order of importance and relevance. Nonetheless, Christ, as the superior officer, and the angel, as the junior officer, worked interdependently and complemented each other. For example, the angel completed the two major assignments given to him. First, he arrived at the sepulcher to roll away the stone from the door of the tomb. Second, he instructed Mary Magdalene and the other women of the role they were to play when he said, "And go quickly, and tell his disciples that he is risen from the dead; and, behold, he goeth before you into Galilee; there shall ye see him: lo, I have told you" (Matthew 28:7). Christ performed His role by appearing to Mary Magdalene and the other women; reaffirming the angel's instruction to tell His disciples to meet Him in Galilee (Matthew 28:10). The women fulfilled their role by carrying the good news to the disciples. Christ, the angel, and the women are modeling how the church and organizations should collaborate and work together as a team.

COALESCING BEHIND A COMMON GOAL

> Matthew 28:2–10; 26:17–19; Genesis 11:1–6; 3:22; Acts 15:2–31; 17:10, 14, 40; 4:32; John 21:5–6; Mark 1:2; 2 Chronicles 5:13

Each character in this story had a separate role but a common goal. No one was trying to compete with or outperform the other. Rather, their focus was concentrated on the goal of seeing that Christ's disciples would meet with Him in Galilee. God's plan was fulfilled because each party to the plan carried out his/her responsibility. The Bible asks, "Can two walk together, except they be agreed?" (Amos 3:3). Walking in agreement among people always yields positive results (Genesis 11:1–6).

In Genesis 1:26, we read, "And God said, let us make man in our image, after our likeness: and let them have dominion over the fish of the sea, and over the fowl of the air, and over the cattle, and over all the earth, and over every creeping thing that creepeth upon the earth." In this verse, God the Father, is speaking for the Trinity (God the Father, God the Son and God the Holy Spirit) using the word *Us*, and the other two important personalities did not disagree with God the Father but coalesced behind the plan.

CPSIA information can be obtained
at www.ICGtesting.com
Printed in the USA
BVHW032230300121
599048BV00015B/109

9 781664 214903